Osprey Modelling • 16

Modelling the F/A-18 Hornet

Geoff Coughlin

Consultant editor Robert Oehler • *Series editors* Marcus Cowper and Nikolai Bogdanovic

First published in 2005 by Osprey Publishing,
Midland House, West Way, Botley, Oxford OX2 0PH, UK
443 Park Avenue South, New York, NY 10016, USA
Email: info@ospreypublishing.com

© 2005 Osprey Publishing Ltd.

ISBN-10: 1-84176-817-0
ISBN-13: 978-1-84176-817-5
Typeset in Monotype Gill Sans and ITC Stone Serif

Editorial by Ilios Publishing, Oxford, UK (www.iliospublishing.com)
Design: Servis Filmsetting Ltd, Manchester, UK
Index by Alison Worthington
Originated by Solidity Graphics, London, UK
Printed and bound in China through Bookbuilders
Typeset in Monotype Gill Sans and ITC Stone Serif

08 09 10 11 12   12 11 10 9 8 7 6 5 4 3

A CIP catalogue record for this book is available from the British Library.

FOR A CATALOGUE OF ALL BOOKS PUBLISHED BY OSPREY PLEASE CONTACT:

NORTH AMERICA
Osprey Direct, C/o Random House Distribution Centre, 400 Hahn Road,
Westminster, MD 21157
E-mail:info@ospreydirect.com

ALL OTHER REGIONS
Osprey Direct, The Book Service Ltd, Distribution Centre, Colchester Road,
Frating Green, Colchester, Essex, CO7 7DW
E-mail: customerservice@ospreypublishing.com

www.ospreypublishing.com

Photographic credits

Unless otherwise indicated, the photographs that appear in this
work were taken by the author.

Acknowledgements and dedication

It is not possible to produce a book such as this without the
support and help of a great many people. At the risk of offending
a generous friend or supporter by a careless omission, special
thanks go to: Jason Cheah at F-4DableModels for supplying
photographs of real TUDM F/A-18D Hornets in Malaysia; Ian
Sayer for his superb help in providing the pictures of real F/A-18A
Top Gun Hornets at NSAWC; Mark Attrill for his excellent
photographs of unusual Hornets featured in the 'special modelling
ideas' chapter; Neil Burkill for access to pictures of his stunning
1/48-scale Hasegawa F/A-18A Hornet; Jonathan Burns and Ian
Taylor for the loan of their great models featuring Hornet scale
models 'in-action'; Les Rawlins for the loan of some good
reference material; and Jay and Gary at Hannants for their
patience and support and in helping to relieve me of copious
amounts of cash!

I dedicate this book to my beautiful daughter, Emily and her
fantastic mother, Sara – I am forever grateful to you both.

Contents

Introduction

The modelling evolution of the F/A-18 Hornet and, more recently the F/A-18E/F Super Hornet, has been slow. Hasegawa and Revell both produced large 1/32-scale models of the Hornet prototype or early production aircraft. These are long-since gone and rarely available now, and were sparsely detailed. For many years, modellers felt frustrated by the lack of a well-produced model in any scale.

Now everything has changed. Suddenly, it seems, we have or are about to see state of the art kit releases in all the major scales addressing the major operational versions of the F/A-18A/B, C/D Hornet or F/A-18E/F Super Hornet. A full summary of the scale models currently available at the time of going to press is included later in this book.

The recent release of the Academy 'superkit' of the F/A-18C Hornet in 1/32 scale stunned many modellers. Academy's intention to release this kit hit the press some four years before the actual event, and many thought this news just too good to be true. Still, four years in the making and 900-plus parts later, this modelling extravaganza is with us and is truly outstanding in most respects. The tooling is very good, as is the level of detail. Fit is generally very good and several sprues are included that feature just about anything the Hornet is likely

Who says that box art doesn't sell? This stunning artwork by Hasegawa's Koike Shigeo graces their F/A-18C release.

Another impressive box-top artwork from Hasegawa's Koike Shigeo – this time for the F/A-18D.

to or could carry in the way of stores and weapons. The complementary release of several outstanding resin and etched-metal super detailing sets from Cutting Edge, Black Box and Eduard have certainly proved irresistible to one person – hence the reason why two of these scale models are featured in this particular book!

We cannot forget Hasegawa though. They have produced some quite superb scale models of the F/A-18C and D with both of these kits featured in your book. The F/A-18C in particular is a joy to build with no fit problems, very detailed metal undercarriage units, a decent cockpit and dropped flaps an option. The latter feature is a real bonus as it is commonly seen on real parked Hornets and too complex to create from a kit with the flaps moulded in the raised position – like the F/A-18E and F models from Italeri.

Whilst on the subject of Italeri, they are the only manufacturer to currently offer the Super Hornet in quarter scale – and their releases of both the E and F have serious shortcomings. These mainly concern the inclusion of a dorsal speed brake, which, although a feature of the earlier Hornet, was deleted on production Es and Fs. The stores pylons are incorrect in shape and, most annoyingly, dropped flaps are not an option. Nonetheless, I have included this kit as one of the five projects in this book to try to show what can be done with the 'only kid on the block'. This is with the aid of the Black Box resin super detail set. Also included are Two Bob's excellent decals for the F/A-18E/F Super Bug and these are terrific in subject matter and quality. By the time you read these words, however, the Revell/Monogram F/A-18E and F should be available.

However, if you want to drop down a scale, Hasegawa has released both the E and F in 1/72 scale – and neat models they are too.

Tools and materials

Every scale modeller is different, and we all use a great variety of tools and materials to achieve the results we want. Here I want to highlight some of the key products that I use and briefly explain why I use them.

Good lighting

There really is no substitute for daylight. However, many of us need to model in the evenings – sometimes into the wee small hours – and to help us there are several options. Until recently I simply used clear blue 'daylight' bulbs that are readily available from stores with domestic retail lighting departments. These give out a natural light which works well most of the time, and are very cost effective solutions to the 'yellow' light problem associated with most household bulbs.

Good lighting is essential – like this superb polarising tube system from Actulite. Clear blue daylight bulbs also work quite well.

Micro Kristal Klear is an ideal adhesive for clear parts and for filling thin gaps, like the fin root shown here.

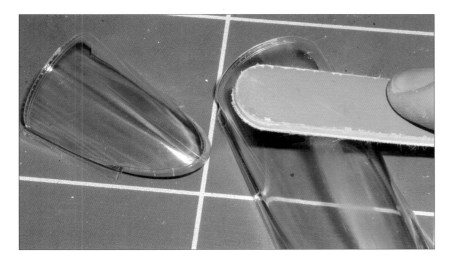

Nail buffers available from cosmetic counters in chemists and pharmacies are excellent sanders and polishers, and are relatively cheap compared to their modelling counterparts.

Micro Mesh comes in packs of assorted grades including 3600 and 12,000 grade and is ideal for final sanding and polishing.

You can also invest in a purpose-made polarised 'daylight' tube light, such as the one produced by Actulite. This is an excellent lighting system that floods your workbench and, in my experience, causes little or no eyestrain. It also offers great coverage across the whole workbench.

Glues and adhesives

Good quality liquid cement is ideal for most tasks during assembly. However I use cyanoacrylate ('superglue') for an increasing number of tasks – apart from attaching etched metal and resin parts. It acts as a good filler, especially if you set it instantly using an 'activator' or 'accelerator' such as those offered by Ripmax and others. Micro Kristal Kleer is ideal for attaching canopies and clear parts as it does not fog or cloud these items.

Paints

There are many paint options available, and the best advice I can give is to try out as many as possible and make your choice for each project. All the main paint manufacturers offer excellent products. I mainly use Xtracolor gloss enamels for camouflage schemes. This dries with a gloss finish, so it is ready to decal straight after drying. Incidentally, I thin this paint with cellulose thinners as it significantly speeds up drying time. Xtracolor matt paints are excellent too and I frequently use them. Poly Scale, Tamiya Color and Aeromaster acrylic are

A decent modeller's razor saw is vital for accurate cutting, especially when trying to remove the resin block from finely detailed accessories (as shown here).

A pin vice drill is superb for enhancing rivets – something I do a lot in 1/32nd scale.

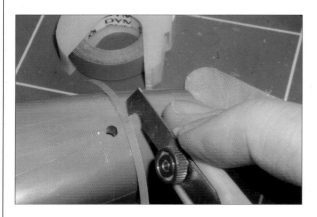

The Olfa P-Cutter is among the best scribing tools on the market as it cleanly removes excess plastic as it cuts. Dymo-type tape is good for guiding the blade around fuselage curves.

Here you can see a small wood chisel from a cheap set I picked up at a hardware store – ideal for plastic and resin, but not much else!

handy when time is at a premium as these paints dry so quickly. Ordinary distilled water is fine for thinning Poly Scale, while Aeromaster and Tamiya have their own thinners. For fine detail painting, for example in the cockpit, I often use Citadel Colour watercolours.

Airbrush work

After about 15 years of hard use, I recently replaced my Badger 200 airbrush with their new 200X – an excellent all round airbrush. I use it mainly for general spraying of the main colours and it needs very little cleaning to keep it in tiptop condition. Badger Spray Away is good for cleaning out enamels at the end of a session. Paint flow is adjusted using a threaded screw attached to the back of the needle.

For more detailed and fine spraying I use a Badger 150 – an excellent double-action airbrush. Double-action simply means that you can adjust the paint and air from the sliding trigger all in one movement.

You simply cannot do without a decent compressor – a good, regular adjustable airflow is as important as the airbrush itself. Revell offer an excellent if somewhat pricey model – but talk to your local suppliers and try and get one or more on loan before you buy if possible.

Sanders and polishers

Nail buffers of various types are widely available in many stores supplying cosmetics and other hand-care products. A wide variety are available and those I have picked up cover just about every modelling task. The dark, slightly bigger ones tend to be stiff but flexible, making them ideally suited to sanding rough seams or when you have filled a gap with superglue.

Cutters and scribers

I use quite a wide selection of scalpels, for progressively finer work. A good quality set of side cutters is essential to remove parts cleanly from the sprue gate. The yellow-handled Olfa P-Cutter with the hooked blade is incredibly useful for rescribing panel lines, especially those difficult curves. This is where the blue Dymo sticky tape comes in, as we shall see in the projects that follow.

Measuring and etched-metal folding tools

Steel rules are designed for measuring, but also come in handy for trapping fuse wire and rolling bent wire to straighten it. The compass pointers are invaluable, as you can save a lot of time using them to measure distance instead of an ungainly rule.

You can just see the compass pointers top right – great for quick and accurate measuring. Notice too the lead foil strips being used as inserts to hide a join seam.

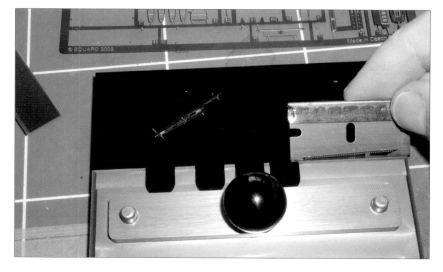

Probably one of the best inventions of recent times for modellers – the Etchmate, a purpose-made precision tool for folding etched metal parts.

'Gunslingers' F/A-18C Hornet, Operation Desert Fox, 1999

Subject:	F/A-18C Bu. No.164200 Hornet flown by Capt. 'Brick' Nelson, CAG, CVW-3 and Capt. 'Killer' Kilkenny, DCAG VFA-105 'Gunslingers'. CAG Bird, USS Enterprise (CVN-65), Operation Desert Fox, 1999	
Skill level:	Intermediate	
Base kit:	Hasegawa No. P26	
Scale:	1/48	
Additional detailing	Eduard F-18C Hornet No. 49 223 (part) sets used:	
Paints:	Xtracolor:	X-135 Dark Compass Grey FS 36320 (upper surfaces)
		X-136 Light Compass Grey FS 36375 (lower surfaces)
		X-107 Radome Tan FS 33613 (tip of radome)
		X-403 Interior Grey FS 36231 (cockpit interior)
		X-141 White FS 37875 (wheel wells)
	Revell:	No.9 Anthracite Black ('black' cockpit areas)
	Tamiya:	Smoke X-19 (undercarriage weathering)
	Polly Scale:	Flat varnish (matt finish)
Decals:	Eagle Strike, Freedom Hornets Part 2. No. 48128	

Overview

As you are probably already aware, the Hasegawa F/A-18C is an excellent kit and an ideal base on which to add a few etched details. The grey plastic is finely tooled, and with the presence of white metal undercarriage parts and a small etched-metal fret that includes the chaff dispensers you are set to begin. I came across the Eduard pre-painted placards and detail sets recently and they are absolutely stunning. The fine, complex, painted detail that they have managed on such small parts – especially for the cockpit and undercarriage – is unbelievable. You simply could not achieve this finesse with a brush and the final effect blows away my previous efforts.

Cockpit detailing

The Eduard set includes well-detailed cockpit decking; this incorporates the canvas netting that is stretched across the rear avionics bay, especially when in flight. You need to cut out the kit moulding but the fit of the etched addition is good.

Interior Grey was sprayed into the cockpit tub, and when dry this was followed with a wash of Tamiya Smoke into the corners and recesses. This is just one way of shading the cockpit tub, but you can apply this approach to the wheel bays in the same way. Go easy with the wash, and when dry, add a slightly lightened shade of the Interior Grey as this really highlights the 3-D effect.

The instrument panels were picked out in very dark grey. Revell No.9 is good for this area as well as the remainder of the 'black' cockpit interior, such as the canopy interior. Black paint is generally too dark and severe. After an hour or so, the dark grey was ready to dry-brush; I generally use a very light grey for this. An old tin of enamel paint is ideal where the heavy paint sediment has settled to the bottom of the tin. Taking an old paintbrush handle, or lengths of sprue, dig up a small amount and let the oil drain off, then wipe the paint onto a tissue. Then, using an old broad brush set aside for the task, smear a small amount of paint onto the bristles and wipe almost all of it off again, so hardly anything is left on the 'dry' bristles. You can then gently, and patiently, brush across the raised detail on the dark-painted parts. Just watch the detail 'pop out' – it looks great when complete. I never try and shortcut this process by adding more paint to save time; although tempting, the finish can be ruined in a stroke.

The main instrument panel is provided in the Eduard pre-painted set and is a small work of art. The pictures overleaf show the finished effect and hopefully speak for themselves. You couldn't hope to achieve this level of accuracy with even the finest paintbrush. The cockpit can then be masked off ahead of the main painting.

The F/A-18C CAG bird of VFA-105 'Gunslingers' finished from the excellent Hasegawa kit. The green and yellow makes a real change and breaks up the somewhat dull Dark and Light Ghost Grey paintwork.

Wheel wells

There is a lot of detail in the Hornet's wheel bays and Hasegawa faithfully reproduces it. You could go much further, but I just feel that unless you pick the model up to show off the undersides, the effort expended here would be all but wasted. However you can make the bays appear to be busier than they are by first pre-shading the whole bay with dark grey or black. Make sure you get into all the corners. When dry, dust on a couple of coats of gloss white and notice how the detail takes on a much busier appearance as areas of 'shadow' are created. It works best if you can keep the head of your airbrush directly above the bay so that most of the paint falls onto the flat, outward-facing surfaces.

Main painting

VFA-105 'Gunslingers' aircraft are painted in the standard Dark Compass Grey (FS 36320) for the upper surfaces and Light Compass Grey (FS 36375) for the undersides. I sprayed the under surfaces first, followed by the slightly darker upper surfaces. I use Xtracolor paints whenever I can, mainly because the gloss paint sprays on evenly and dries with a high gloss finish, ideal for decaling. I also find that by adding a little cellulose thinners to the Xtracolor paint it dries much quicker than thinning with anything else. Do make sure you spray in a well-ventilated space and wear an appropriate particle resistant facemask – it really is worth it. Don't forget to mask off the small front section of the nose cone as this is painted Radome Tan (FS 33613).

Here the etched canopy sills are quickly and accurately folded using the Etchmate.

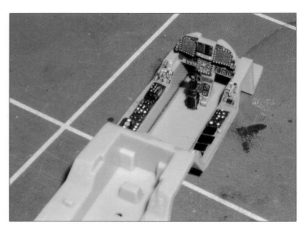

This shot shows the very nice Eduard pre-painted etched cockpit detail in place.

A pin vice drill is a handy tool to create lots of holes around the section to be removed.

The small canvas deck section behind the ejection seat comes away to be replaced with a much finer etched item.

Another shot of the completed cockpit tub showing off the Eduard set.

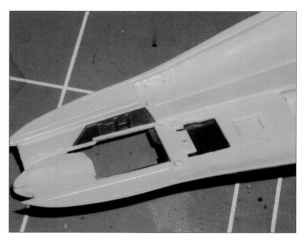

Here you can see the etched replacement sidewalls added to the upper cockpit – always dry-test fit first.

The very neat Eduard canvas cover replacement fits snugly into the recess.

The cockpit begins to take shape and is a considerable upgrade from the original moulded kit detail.

The engine intake vents can be replaced with very subtle etched items – the chisel is used to remove the moulded detail.

You can just make out the new individual vent splitter plates – as yet unpainted.

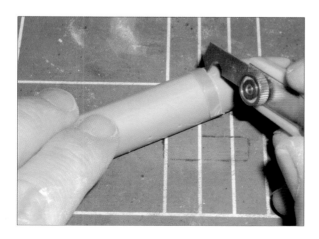

Once you've sanded down the seam left from joining the fuel tank halves, Dymo tape and an Olfa P-Cutter make good the panel line detail.

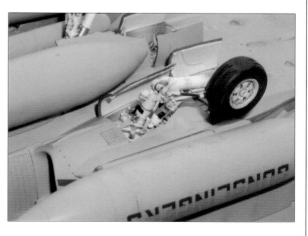

The wheel wells are fairly busy with moulded-in detail and look fine when the main gear is attached.

The finished model showing the very colourful decals from Eagle Strike.

An interesting shot showing the interior of the speed brake housing. Note the Interior Grey colour and small coloured details.

Weathering

What is very noticeable on US Navy carrier aircraft is the way that the paint scheme is touched up, especially around removable panels. Small areas of freshly added paint are very clear and this looks very convincing if done well on scale models. I did some of this over the upper surfaces in particular by using a slightly lighter shade of the topcoat. This was added using my Badger 150, with the paint very well thinned and the compressor pressure turned right down to about 8psi. Test the flow of paint on a piece of old card first to check the flow and then come in very close to the model, about 0.75in. or 1cm. Also be careful not to stop, as it is very easy to create a pool of paint that is difficult to remove. With practice the effect can be quite convincing but I am definitely still on a learning curve with this one!

Undercarriage

Hasegawa supply very nice white metal undercarriage units and while your paint dries you can turn your attention to building these up. Much as I did with the wheel bays, it pays to pre-shade the assembled units with dark grey or black

The finished model again – but notice the extended crew entry ladder, open canopy to show off the interior, and display base.

The rear left side – note the 'slime lights' and offset rudders. The latter are often seen both canted inwards – especially on take off.

paint first. The gloss white follows and it's really noticeable how much depth the legs have – again creating a good 3D effect. When completely dry you can add the stunning stencil placards from the Eduard set. These stencils are very obvious on real F/A-18s and are a fantastic addition to the kit – the icing on the cake for the finished model.

Decals and finishing off

Not only is the subject original, but the quality of the Eagle Strike decals is also first rate in terms of printing accuracy and thinness of the carrier film. They went on superbly using a little Micro Set and Sol decal softening solutions.

Hornets definitely seem to have a very flat finish, even when they've been deployed at sea for some time. Polly Scale flat varnish is excellent for reproducing this, spraying on easily and drying very flat.

Dark grey pastel chalk along the panel lines helps to bring them to life and, in my view, is more convincing on modern jets like the Hornet than a wash with ink.

In focus: the canopy

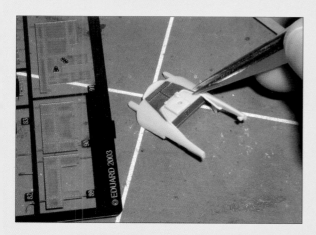

Some nicely tooled etched items add detail to the rear canopy deck.

Micromesh Polishing Cloth

Pack Contents

1 x 3600 Grade
1 x 4000 Grade
1 x 6000 Grade
1 x 8000 Grade
1 x 12000 Grade

1 x Foam rubber
polishing pad

Micro Mesh is an essential tool when preparing canopies because of the fine grades supplied in the pack.

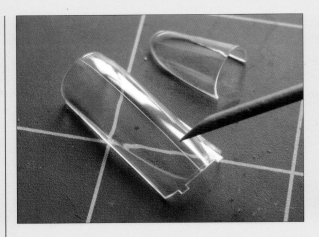

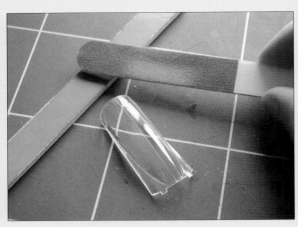

You can see me pointing out the mould seam line that needs to be removed from the kit canopy.

First, gently sand away the seam line using a medium grit nail buffer.

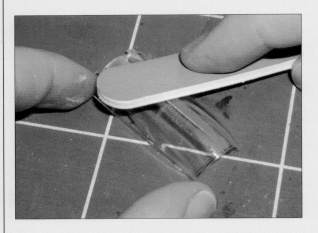

Secondly, use the slightly smoother (often white) grade to remove most of the scratches.

Micro Mesh comes next, which begins to restore the shine – note the use of a firm foam block as a grip.

The final stage of preparation is to use MER car polish applied using a very soft cloth and then buffed up – but go easy to avoid crazing the clear part.

The finished canopy. I wash my canopies in warm soapy water to remove any traces of polish before painting.

'Sidewinders' F/A-18C Hornet

Subject:	F/A-18C Hornet Bu No. 163446, flown by Capt. Stufflebeem CAG and Capt. Cuninghame Dep. CAG VFA-86 'Sidewinders'. USS George Washington (CVN-73), Miami Ft. Lauderdale visit, 1996	
Skill level:	Intermediate	
Base kit:	Academy No. 2191	
Scale:	1/32	
Additional detailing sets used:	Reheat Seat Buckle and Harness (RH04) M.V. Products real lens for nose leg light (L 149)	
Paints:	Xtracolor:	X-135 Dark Compass Grey FS 36320 (upper surfaces) X-136 Light Compass Grey FS 36375 (underside) X-107 Radome Tan FS 33613 (tip of nose radome) X-403 Interior Grey FS 36231 (cockpit interior) X-141 White FS 37875 (wheel wells, wheel hubs, u/c door interior)
	Revell:	No.9 Anthracite Black (seats, canopy interior, HUD)
	Tamiya:	Smoke X-19 (weathering wheels, u/c legs)
	Humbrol:	27004 Metalcote Gun Metal (afterburner cans) 174 Matt Red (edges undercarriage doors)
	Polly Scale:	505350 Nato Tri Black (tyres) Flat varnish
Decals:	Eagle Strike 'Freedom Hornets' Part II (32050)	

Overview

By any standards this recent release by Academy is simply stunning. Over four years in the design stage, its 900 parts offer the F/A-18 Hornet builder both quality and quantity. Unquestionably the best aspects of the kit are: generally well moulded parts; the range of stores options included; accuracy; white metal inserts to strengthen the undercarriage units; dropped flaps; stencil decals for aircraft and stores; and a comprehensive and helpful instruction book. There are a few drawbacks and these include: sink marks on forward fuselage sides; and the fit of the engine air intakes (you'll need filler here and it's difficult to replace some of lost detail due to sanding).

My intention with this build is to try to show what can be achieved simply by using the parts supplied (with the exception of the decals and seat buckles). There are several excellent resin and etched super-detail sets now available and some of these are included in the F/A-18A 'Aggressor' project on page 45ff.

Main construction

The cockpit assembly comprises a very neatly moulded tub and instruments with integral net cover over the avionics bay behind the ejection seat. I painted the net a slightly different shade of dark grey and shaded it with pastels to make

The finished model sporting the superb decals for VFA-86 'Sidewinders'.

it look more realistic. I simply sprayed the main Interior Grey colour onto the flat areas of the tub and instruments; notice how this stands out slightly from the darker grey plastic. This is in effect a simple pre-shading technique and is later enhanced by spraying Tamiya Smoke into the corners and recesses. The small raised knobs and switches are well tackled by Academy and stand out when dry-brushed with an off-white or very light grey paint. Good references are essential here (see the *Further Reading* chapter). The F/A-18C cockpit is relatively uncluttered with the main instrument panel being dominated by the three square CRT (Cathode Ray Tube) digital displays. When the aircraft systems are shut down these look dark – a very deep green–purple. I added plenty

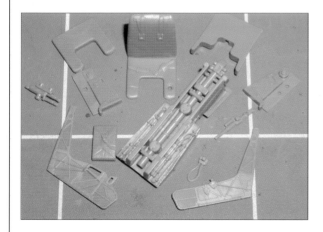

The kit representation of the Martin Baker SJU-5/6 ejection seat is very respectable. Here the unassembled parts are displayed.

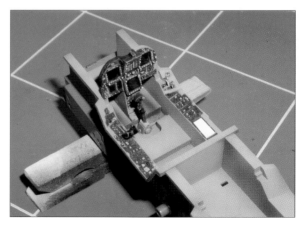

The cockpit nears completion. Academy have done a pretty good job detailing the F/A-18C 'office'.

The completed seat, painted and dry-brushed. The harness is made from metal foil and etched buckles come from an old Reheat etched-metal set.

The seat from the other side. There is always more you can add, especially in this bigger scale (see the Academy kit project on page 45ff.)

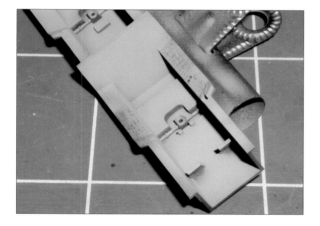

The cockpit tub received a coat of dark grey ahead of the much lighter Interior Grey that was then ghosted on, leaving shadows in the recesses.

With the addition of the completed seat, the cockpit really looks the part.

A right-side view this time. As far as cockpits go, the Hornet office is pretty colourful. The yellow/black warning placards are mostly painted yellow foil.

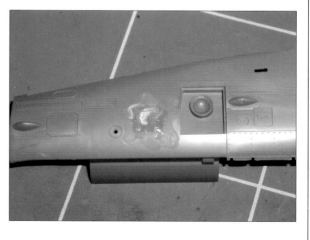

You'll need to fill a couple of panels on each side of the nose for an F/A-18C. The instructions help, as do the plans in the magnificent Daco Publications pictorial reference (see page 73).

The fit of the intakes left a little to be desired. The gaps were filled with superglue and sanded; then re-scribed, as you can see.

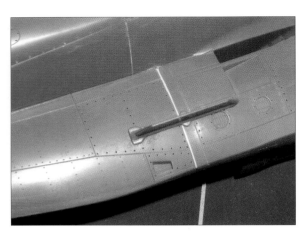

The LEX on the port side left a thin gap where it mated to the upper fuselage. A thin piece of plastic card cut down to size filled the gap nicely, secured in place using liquid poly.

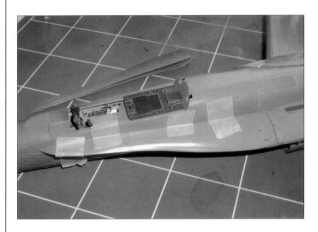

The LEXs are a good fit to the fuselage sides – you just need to be very accurate when placing them and taping them up tightly is a good idea. When all is dry, any thin gaps can be effectively filled using PVA glue or Micro Kristal Kleer.

Rivets are marked on the clear canopy parts. They look even better if you drill shallow holes in each recess – they stand out when painted and create more interest on the finished model.

of Tamiya Clear Green over the grey and they looked quite good – maybe a little light, but then again I wanted them to be seen when the finished cockpit is viewed.

The Martin Baker SJU-5A ejection seat is well moulded, and by adding some scratch-built harness straps using lead or other metal foil and the Reheat buckles they can look pretty convincing. Another option is to replace this part with a resin seat.

Revell No.9 Anthracite Black is an excellent dark grey paint to use for the 'black' cockpit interior areas and seat/instrument covers. See the captions that accompany the pictures for full details of how the cockpit comes together – but note that the seat is best left off until the end of the project to prevent damage.

The finished tub attaches to the nose gear bay, and the instructions tell you to attach the nose gear leg at this stage. My suggestion is leave it off and trim the locating tabs later to get it to slot into place. This is very straightforward and avoids lots of masking and potential damage to what is a delicately detailed sub assembly.

While this dries you can turn your attention to filling the sink marks on the forward side of the nose sections (if you have these flaws). A small amount of superglue does the trick, and this can be sanded and the area rescribed with an Olfa P-Cutter.

You'll also need to decide whether to add the 600,000-candlepower searchlight to the front port side if building a Canadian, Kuwaiti, Swiss or Finnish machine, as these have this fitted. I chose to drill out several of the rivets using a 0.3mm pin vice drill because I think it improves the final look of the aircraft when fully weathered.

The main sub assemblies comprising the upper and lower centre fuselage, nose halves and separate side panels all go together pretty well – but, be careful to make sure everything is lined up so as to avoid unnecessary filling later on. The leading edge extensions (or LEXs) are nicely moulded but the starboard one left a gap when mated to the fuselage. This was easily fixed by running PVA/wood glue or Micro Kristal Kleer into the gap, wiping the excess off immediately with a damp tissue. This technique was also useful for eliminating the hairline gaps created when the twin fins were attached. The canopy and windscreen benefit from drilling out the rivets.

The wheel bays are busy with detail and I rarely add any extra detail when they are moulded like this. There is a lot of cabling and other detail on the real aircraft but I figured that when this large model was finished I was not going to start picking it up and showing off the underside – just too risky. I opted to spend extra time detailing what would be seen when the model was standing on its legs.

Radar

Academy has produced a very good representation of the AN/APG-65 multi-mode, pulse Doppler radar mounted in the nose cone, which can be displayed open. Again, references are helpful, but the kit instructions go a long way to help finish the area realistically. The real radar has several extra wires and cables protruding from the side of the set and a little extra effort here can pay dividends with the finished results.

Wing fold

One of the characteristics of the F/A-18 Hornet is that when parked on carrier decks the wings are almost always raised in the folded position. The manufacturer has captured this well with a good wing fold option. The wing tips need to be carefully removed with a sharp scalpel but with care the operation should run smoothly. Each step of how to do this is carefully explained in the instruction book.

Afterburner/reheat cans

There are many ways to achieve a realistic finish in this area, and several different options have been covered

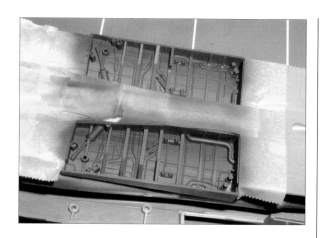

As you can see, the wheel wells are quite detailed. You can always add some of the wiring looms. Here the bays are pre-shaded using Anthracite Grey.

The AN/APG-65 radar is supplied separately in the kit and makes up into a nice unit that is pretty complete.

You'll need to decide early on whether to have your F/A-18C displayed with the wing tips folded. The instructions are clear and the end result is effective – ideal for a diorama.

A pleasing picture of the finished model showing just how much detail Academy have put into their tooling – great credit to them for this.

throughout this book. In this project I used Humbrol Metalcote Gun Metal. It sprays on beautifully and is ready to be buffed lightly in an hour or so. Go easy and build up the effect you want by lightly buffing with a clean, soft cloth. I use a really soft antiques duster and this works well. The finishing touches can be made using various shades of brown pastel dust applied with a short, stubby-bristled, dry paintbrush.

A close-up of the port wing and load. Academy give you all the stencil data for the stores provided in the kit and most of it is very accurate. You'll need to allow plenty of time for applying all the hundreds of decals to your model.

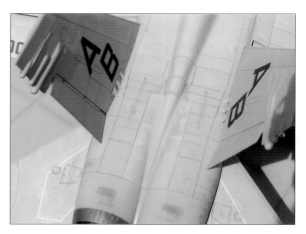

Classic Hornet – the tell-tale streaking back from the two vent holes forward and between the fins. The residue is often a yellowish colour – added here with pastels and applied using a very small, thin brush.

In focus: undercarriage units

The main undercarriage units are excellent and look really good when finished. The white metal parts are models in themselves! Cocktail sticks and bulldog clips help secure everything for painting.

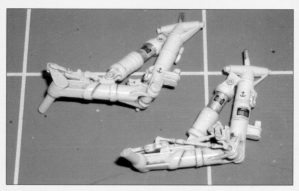

The main units are nearly finished – note the Eduard placards and kit decals as well as the Tamiya Smoke wash.

The main gear units complete. Dark grey paint and pastels help to create that rubber look – all very rewarding when finished.

Nose gear leg this time. The large landing/taxi light dominates the front upper section. Tamiya clear colours also come into their own.

All three units together, to help provide you with reference. They all fit into their slots in the bays with little difficulty.

You can see the finished effect works well enough. It's useful to complete all the remaining tasks underneath before going on to finish the upper airframe.

The starboard side, showing the AGM-84E missile to good effect. Notice too how the simulated concrete base helps set the model off.

Painting, decals and finishing

I used Hannants Xtracolor paints for this model: Dark Compass Grey (FS 36320 Dark Ghost Gray) for the upper surfaces and Light Compass Grey (FS 36375 Light Ghost Gray) for the undersides. The nose tip was done in Radome Tan (FS 33613). The high gloss finish is ideal for applying the decals later on. I couldn't resist the fantastic scheme for the CAG '400' aircraft of VFA-86 'Sidewinders'. The orange and black scheme looks really impressive on the completed model, but there are several aftermarket decal sheets now available in 1/32 scale if you fancy something a bit different to the manufacturer's offering.

One of my favourite pictures. This low-down angle shot gives an idea of size and proportion of the F/A-18C Hornet.

F/A-18D Hornet, Royal Malaysian Air Force

Subject:	F/A-18D Hornet '07' of Tentera Diraja Malaysia (TUDM – Royal Malaysian Air Force) No. 18 Squadron, Butterworth Malaysia, 2003	
Skill level:	Advanced	
Base kit:	Hasegawa, kit no. PT.3	
Scale:	1/48th	
Additional detailing sets used:	Black Box F/A-18D Cockpit set (48060) Eduard F/A-18 Hornet pre-painted placards (FE196) Eduard Remove Before Flight tags (73 008)	
Paints:	Xtracolor:	X-130 Gunship Grey FS 36118 (overall) X-137 Light Gull Grey FS 36375 (radome tip – note, not Radome Tan) X-408 Matt Zinc Chromate (slime lights) X-403 Interior Grey FS 36231 (cockpit interior) X-141 White FS 37875 (wheel wells, interior of afterburner cans)
	Revell:	No.9 Anthracite Black (seats, cockpit, canopy interior, afterburner cans) SM371 (most dry-brushing)
	Humbrol:	27003 Polished Steel (titanium band ahead of afterburner cans) 174 Matt Red (edges of undercarriage doors)
	Tamiya:	Smoke X-19 (weathering undercarriage legs, wheels)
	Polly Scale:	F505350 NATO Tri Black (tyres) Flat varnish
Decals:	F-4Dable Models	

The finished model looks very smart in the Gunship Grey scheme – a nice alternative to the usual greys.

The real aircraft – a picture gallery

ABOVE Some invaluable pictures of the real thing. You can just see the Light Gull Grey radome tip and overall Gunship Grey scheme. (Jason Cheah)

RIGHT Although a bit distant, it's nice to see that 06 has been cleaned up for the air display. A very neat scheme indeed. (Jason Cheah)

LEFT Right side of the nose clearly illustrating the roundel colours – reversed in error on delivery of the aircraft and changed to the correct order here. (Jason Cheah)

BELOW Left side of the nose. You can just see the RBF tags and engine intake covers. (Jason Cheah)

Nice picture of the left fin, slime lights and smart three-colour national insignia. (Jason Cheah)

Close up of 07 – note the stencil data and colour of the slime lights. (Jason Cheah)

Under the tail this time showing the colours of the tail hook, stencil data and afterburner/reheat cans. (Jason Cheah)

You can just make out the bulges on the leading edges of the main gear doors – aft fairings for the twin chaff-flare dispensers. (Jason Cheah)

Excellent! I just love the twin FOD cushions that sit inside the jet pipes. Note too the trailing RBF tags – which will be added to the forthcoming F/A-18F build. (Jason Cheah)

The twin stores racks are empty here but TUDM aircraft can carry a wide range of stores. (Jason Cheah)

Overview

The inspiration for this project arose from the excellent decal sheet from F-4 Dable Models, which features a Royal Malaysian Air Force (TUDM) F/A-18D. The eight aircraft delivered in July 1997 wear a very smart Gunship Grey (FS 36118) camouflage scheme overall. The small national markings and roundels break up the grey and the effect is complete with a fair amount of weathering. The instructions included in the pack provide a wealth of information that you'll need to modify the kit that represents an early Lot 11/12 aircraft and bring it up to 'Late Lot' standard. Few decal sheets are as helpful and none of the modifications is too difficult, as you'll see in the following pages. The Hasegawa kit used in this project is almost identical to the F/A-18C described in the opening chapter and so I will try to avoid being repetitive in this section.

Cockpit detailing and valuable resources

I couldn't resist the Black Box resin conversion set for producing an ATARS F/A-18D. If you discard the replacement resin nose, just about everything else is usable – you just need to follow both the decal and Black Box instruction sheets and use the excellent Daco publications reference book (see *Further reading*). The latter contains all the colour cockpit photographs you could wish for. Another very useful resource is F-4Dable Models own website (www.F4DableModels.com). This features pictures of the real aircraft and has a very useful newsletter to download.

The resin cockpit is designed with separate front and rear tubs, but they are moulded very neatly to fit onto locating pins, and position positively within the kit nose section.

I sprayed the tub and other cockpit parts dark grey (Revell No.9) as a method of pre-shading and when dry added the Interior Grey. You can lightly spray the grey at right angles onto the flat surfaces, in this way leaving darker areas in the recesses that are shadowed. The next step is to carefully hand paint the instrument panels with very dark grey; any touching up of the Interior Grey base coat can be done after the instruments. The next stage involves dry-brushing all the beautiful raised detail and I use a very light grey – white is a bit too severe with too much contrast, and rarely looks authentic.

My tip here is to add the tiny resin throttle quadrants after the cockpit is finished – otherwise they are likely to go 'walkabout' during the dry-brushing stage! The next stage involves adding all the additional micro detail such as placards (Eduard set), warning signs and markings and coloured knobs. The coloured metal foil you get on the tops of wine bottles is excellent for these tasks and it's one of the most enjoyable modelling tasks for me.

I had no fit problems with the Black Box resin parts and they greatly to the basic airframe. The finishing touch to the cockpit is the addition of the hoses that are prominent down the left side of each crewmember.

Additions

The F-4DableModels decal sheet lists all the small changes and additions that you need to make, but the good news is that many of them, like the new aerials, GPS dome antenna and coaming in between the pilot and rear seat are included by Black Box. What you don't get in this set are the twin Chaff/flare dispensers – so I scratchbuilt them from thick plastic card.

Using superglue, I attached the pre-cut, shaped and drilled dispensers on the underside of each intake. Micro Kristal Kleer is ideal for fairing in the parts so that they look like integral parts of the airframe.

Main painting

As you can see, the entire model is sprayed Gunship Grey, and I used Hannants Xtracolor gloss enamel. I slightly darkened the base coat and added a second,

(continued on page 33)

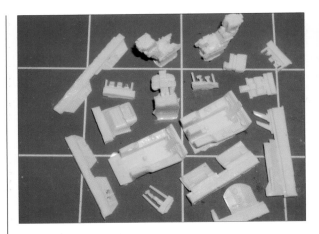

The Black Box resin detail set laid out and looking a bit daunting. Nonetheless, it all fits pretty well and makes a huge difference to the finished cockpit.

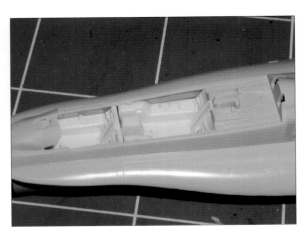

Here you can see the new tub sitting snugly in the upper fuselage – just being test-fitted at this stage.

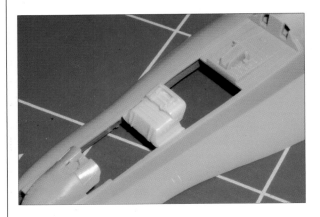

The rear instrument panel coaming fits neatly between the front and rear cockpits.

The completed cockpit is very rewarding. The resin seats make all the difference.

Again the completed cockpit from the rear. Note the large green CRT screens that dominate the instrument panels.

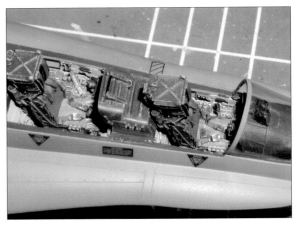

The finished cockpit from the right. A nice touch can be to add some rolled up RBF tags and/or put them in their correct locations.

The final touch is to add the hoses that are prominent on the left side of each seat, connecting down to the rear of the left instrument panels.

Rear and right view of the completed cockpit. Note the dark Anthracite Grey overall colour – much more realistic than pure black.

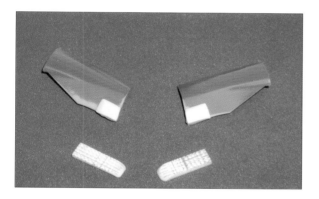

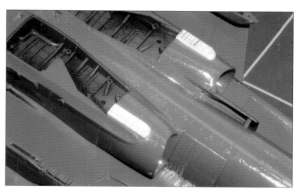

The main addition you need to add apart from the Black Box set bits are the twin chaff/flare dispensers. These are scratched here from thick plastic card faired into the fuselage and leading edges of the main gear doors.

The new chaff flare dispensers are in place and just need spraying. Take a look at F-4Dable Model's website for more references on the real parts.

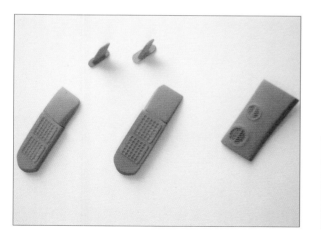

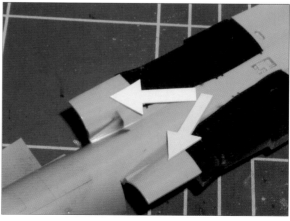

Jason Cheah managed to get some test shots to me just before completing this book, of the new resin parts to help make a TUDM F/A-18D – available from F-4Dable Models.

Two vents on the underside of the fuselage (arrowed here) need to be removed.

In-focus: afterburner/reheat cans

The reheat cans are first painted an off-white colour inside – in keeping with the later General Electric engines.

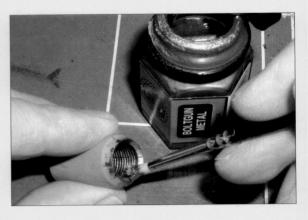

The inner tubular section receives a coat of silver, followed by a bronze colour wash from Citadel Colour.

The inner sections of each jet pipe await mating to the outer cans, but the cans need spraying first.

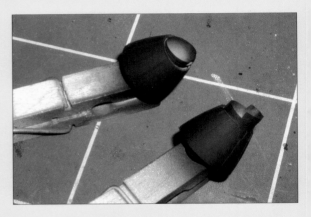

You have several options for creating realistic metallic reheat cans. In this instance I've used Revell No.9 Anthracite Black for the base colour followed by graphite pencil dust worked into the surface with a small stubby brush. Humbrol Metalcote Gun Metal is another good option.

To give a realistic worn finish I then work in brown pastel dust, ensuring that it collects in the recesses.

One of the completed jet exhaust cans.

The finished article. Note the overall dark metallic appearance typical of F/A-18 Hornet afterburner cans.

I like this picture, showing the completed reheat cans in place on the finished F/A-18D. The decals have gone down well too – all credit to F-4Dable Models for a quality decal product.

slightly lighter shade to the centre of most upper surface panels to help simulate weathering to the airframe. Another slight difference with the TUDM machines is the colour of the radome tip. Normally this is left unpainted or painted Radome Tan, but on these aircraft the shade is more like Light Gull Grey.

Touches of detail

Eduard now produces some beautifully pre-painted Remove Before Flight (RBF) tags that greatly enhance any finished model. The only problem seems to be their size. The quarter-scale items seem about right for 1/32nd scale and the 1/72nd parts just right for 1/48th – so the 1/72nd scale items were used here. The tyres need pastel chalk dusted on with an old brush and for this I used a light grey pastel.

A very pleasing picture of the finished model set against an airfield backdrop.

The finished left tail fin. Note the subtle streaking using pastels, rivets enhanced with a pin vice drill early on in construction, and replacement 'slime lights' from lead foil.

Undercarriage

Hasegawa supply the same, very nice, white metal undercarriage units that are featured in their 'C' offering. While your paint dries you can turn your attention to building these up. Much as I did with the wheel bays, it pays to pre-shade the assembled units with dark grey or black paint first. The gloss white follows and it's really noticeable how much depth the legs have – again creating a good 3-D effect. When completely dry you can add the stunning stencil placards from the Eduard set. These stencils are very obvious on real F/A-18s and are a fantastic addition to the kit.

Decals

The F-4DableModels decals are very good quality indeed, and adhere well. I used only small amounts of decal setting solution from Microscale. Not only is the subject original but the quality is also first rate in terms of printing accuracy and thinness of the carrier film.

Finishing off

TUDM Hornets seem to have a very definite 'flat' finish, even though they are not deployed on carriers. Polly Scale Flat varnish is excellent – spraying on easily and drying very flat – just what you need.

The completed nose section. The radome tip painted in Light Gull Grey stands out. You can just see the tubing attaching the ejection seats to the left side instrument panels.

'Black Aces' F/A-18F Super Hornet

Subject:	F/A-18F (Bu.165877) '101', Super Hornet flown by Capt. 'Stubby' P.R. Cleary, CO, VFA-41 and Cdr. 'Sheboy' K.R. Whitesell, XO, VFA-41 'Black Aces'; USS Nimitz	
Skill level:	Advanced	
Base kit:	Italeri, No. 2619	
Scale:	1/48th	
Additional detailing sets used:	Black Box F/A-18F Super Hornet cockpit set No. 48066	
	Eduard F-18C Hornet No. 49 223 (part)	
	Eduard RBF tags 73 008 (more accurate than 1/48)	
	M.V. Products clear lenses: No. L149 (nose gear)	
	No. LS23 right fin tip	
	Hasegawa Weapons set: US missiles and gun pods No. 48-3	
Paints:	Xtracolor:	X-135 Dark Compass Grey FS 36320 (upper surfaces)
		X-136 Light Compass Grey FS 36375 (underside)
		X-107 Radome Tan FS 33613 (tip of nose radome)
		X-403 Interior Grey FS 36231 (cockpit interior)
		X-141 White FS 37875 (wheel wells, wheel hubs, u/c door interior)
	Revell:	9 Anthracite Black (seats, canopy interior, HUD)
		96 Red (fin tips)
	Tamiya:	Smoke X-19 (weathering wheels, u/c legs)
	Humbrol:	109 matt blue (AIM-9L body)
		27003 Metalcote Polished Steel (AIM-9L heads, nose cannon port)
		174 matt Red (edges undercarriage doors)
	Polly Scale:	505350 NATO Tri Black (tyres)
		Flat varnish
Decals:	Two Bobs, F/A-18F Super Bugs No. 48-041	

Overview

No modelling manual covering the Hornet could be complete without at least one project featuring the Super Bug – in this case the F/A-18F two-seat variant. At first glance the Super Hornet is very similar to its predecessor, the F/A-18 Hornet, or, as it has more recently become known, the Legacy Hornet. At the time of writing, at least one and perhaps as many as three 1/48th-scale models featuring the single seat F/A-18E and twin seat 'F' were scheduled for release. Revell-Monogram are due to release both versions and Trumpeter also have a Super Hornet listed for future release.

At present, Italeri provide the only offerings, having released both the 'E' and 'F'. The F/A-18F is the basis for my project here, and I know from talking to colleagues and fellow modellers that many of them have the model either

Low down shot of the completed Italeri kit. It is hard work, but well worth the effort.

The cockpit nears completion. Note the seats are left off until right at the end of the project to avoid damage.

assembled or waiting to be built. This is not surprising; the Italeri kit is a challenge, but if you make a few amendments to correct some over-simplified tooling you can achieve a decent finished scale model. With the addition of the superb Black Box resin cockpit everything starts to look very good. But it doesn't end there – Two Bobs has released a fantastic decal sheet featuring aircraft from VFA-41. This addition sealed the kit's fate – it had to be built!

Cockpit detailing

The Black Box resin cockpit is very delicately moulded and faithfully replicates the interior of the F/A-18F. The front cockpit is very similar in layout to the F/A-18E single seater with the five large display panels. The rear cockpit main instrument panel differs slightly, the second control column being omitted and with a small hand controller located forward on each side panel. The latest NACES SJU-17 ejection seat is also included in the Black Box set, easily distinguishable from predecessor models by having a flat top on the headrest with moulded diagonal cross.

Here you can see the completed Black Box cockpit set installed in the aircraft. This is a good resin aftermarket set.

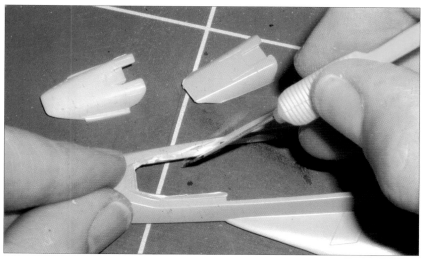

Black Box provide a neat replacement pilot's instrument shroud, so the kit's moulding needs to be removed – follow the instructions here.

You need excellent reference material to do these sets justice and the In Detail and Scale publication on the F/A-18E and F/A-18F is an absolute must for the job. It features colour pictures of both front and rear cockpits. The colour scheme applied to each is essentially the same as for previous Legacy Hornets and is fully described elsewhere in this book – so I'll focus on other key areas here. The main task is to align the cockpit tub correctly with the Italeri forward fuselage halves. Black Box do give suggested measurements and this is very helpful. It is worth double and triple checking to make sure that when you fit the instrument panels (which I only did after the completed tub had been installed) everything is aligned and going to look right. To aid tub and fuselage alignment I added two thin strips of plastic for the tub to sit on, which helped a lot. I also found it useful to support the front of the tub with a small plug between it and the top of the nose gear bay. The SJU-17 seats can be painted later on – always add these at the very final stages of your project to avoid unnecessary damage.

In focus: ejection seats

Stage 1 – remove the seats from their resin moulding blocks and mount for spraying – in this case, using Revell No.9.

Stage 2 – hand-painting all the main colours seen on the NACES SJU-17 seat.

Stage 3 – dry-brush the seat and add a thin wash using Tamiya Smoke before adding any final touches like ejection handles.

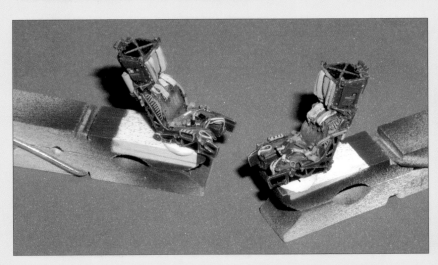

Corrections and modifications

There are a number of details that need attention and the accompanying pictures show you the necessary steps. What follows is a brief summary:

- Outboard weapon stations: these need to be angled both outward by 3.5 degrees and away from the centreline by 4 degrees.
- Inner and centre main wing weapons pylons: angle away from the centre-line by 4 degrees.
- Reshape the inner and centre main wing pylons; those fitted to the Super Hornet are different to earlier versions
- Eliminate the upper fuselage air brake; this is omitted on the Super Hornet.
- Add the 'pizza box' to the upper nose section; LRIP-II aircraft after Bu No: 165660 have the familiar 'pizza-box' shaped fairing in front of the windscreen.
- Scribe a new panel line down the length of the fuselage, as shown. I didn't have access to full scale plans, so check your references for other panel lines that may need attention.
- LEX spoilers and vents: the vents ahead of the spoilers are a very poor fit – as are the spoilers – and careful filling, sanding and re-scribing is required to produce an acceptable result.
- V-shaped Standoff cable guard: scratchbuild this small addition and add it below the rear fuselage ahead of the tail hook.
- Navigation lights: you need to scratchbuild these for the inner leading edge root of the AIM-9 wing-tip launch rails. I used small pieces of metal foil painted with clear red and blue. For the small lights on top of each LEX, fill the marked kit recesses and use foil for the small clear sections.
- Undercarriage: the units are all oversimplified and reference to the *In Detail and Scale* guide will highlight some additions that you can make.

Main painting

VFA-41 'Black Aces' aircraft are painted in the standard Dark Compass Grey (FS 36320) for the upper surfaces and Light Compass Grey (FS 36375) for the undersides. I sprayed the under surfaces first, followed by the slightly darker upper surfaces. Xtracolor was again used as it gives a lovely gloss finish for the decals. The interesting colour for this aircraft ('101') centres on the 'red' fin tips. I used a Revell red, No 96. It matches the darker red given in the Two Bob's decal sheet quite well. Don't forget to mask off the small front section of the nose cone as this is painted Radome Tan (FS 33613).

Undercarriage

The picture on page 42 shows the completed undercarriage units, and the additional detail. You need to add an extra retraction arm down the front of each main gear leg as this is omitted in the kit. Watch out too for smaller details because on first glance the undercarriage units appear to be the same as that fitted to the Legacy Hornets. This is not the case – probably because the Super Hornet is approximately 25 per cent bigger than its predecessor, thus forcing a redesign of the undercarriage. The main addition, apart from the extra retraction arms for the main gear legs, is to add a realistic-looking lens for the nose gear unit – MV Lenses are ideal.

Decals

Two Bob's decals are excellent, adhering cleanly with no silvering of the thin carrier film. The quality of the printing is first rate in terms of accuracy. Several items are provided as two-part decals so that you can achieve perfect alignment. They went on superbly, using a little Micro Set and Sol decal softening solutions.

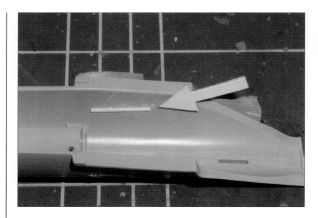

It's important to correctly align the replacement cockpit tub. The instructions are clear and here I am using plastic strip guide rails to help.

Remove the airbrake – I am using superglue to fill the small gaps where the airbrake has been glued in place. The superglue dries hard and the area can be re-scribed.

The main assemblies are a poor fit and gaps need to be filled – again superglue works well. Try using an activator or glue accelerator to set the glue immediately.

The panel lines are simplified in the Italeri kit and so rivets are drilled out to help create a more interesting look to the finished model.

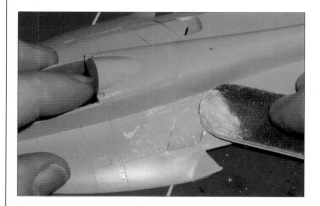

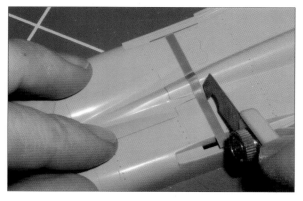

The LEX vents are a very poor fit and are best glued in place, filled and re-scribed. In fact the vents and leading-edge slat spoilers that fit into the wing roots are invariably closed when Super Hornets are parked. The LEX vents are totally flush when closed and so lend themselves to re-scribing.

Here you can see me using an Olfa P-Cutter to replace panel lines damaged during sanding. Dymo tape is used to guide the blade.

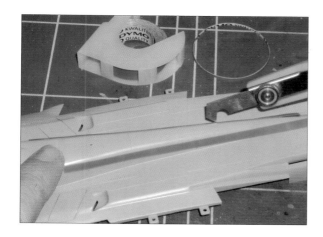

A long panel line runs down each side of the upper fuselage and is being added here. Check out pictures of the real aircraft for placing.

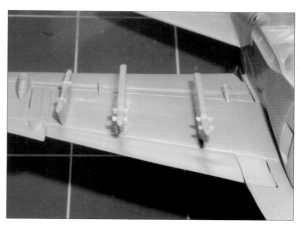

The under-wing pylons on the F/A-18E/F actually deflect outwards from the centreline by 4 degrees. The outer pylon under each wing also tilts away from the centreline by 3.5 degrees – all just visible in this shot.

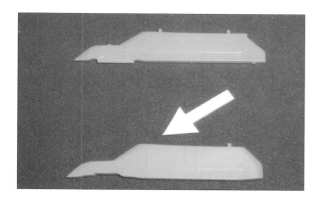

The four inner wing pylons need reworking to a more accurate shape. The 'new' pylon is shown arrowed.

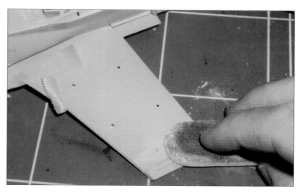

By filling the front pylon pin location holes, the pylons can be swivelled out by 4 degrees. Just remove the front pins from the pylons and keep the rear pins. I had to open up the location holes slightly using a round rat-tail file, so that the pins would fit.

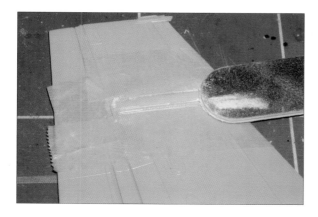

The wing-fold hinge is quite inaccurate and was sanded away here and reinstated using metal foil.

The new 'pizza-box' fairing stuck down with superglue and shaped to fit – made from a thick piece of plastic card.

ABOVE AND RIGHT Blu Tac stationary putty is ideal for rolling into thin lengths and used as a mask to get a thin

feathered edge – but remove immediately after spraying to avoid staining.

The undercarriage units are simplified and here fuse wire and etched-brass scrap is used to detail each item.

The left side this time showing the added detail.

The completed main gear units with additional retraction arms just visible at the front of each leg.

The kit AIM-9L Sidewinders are OK, but the Hasegawa items are better tooled – note blue inert drill round to be just that little bit different.

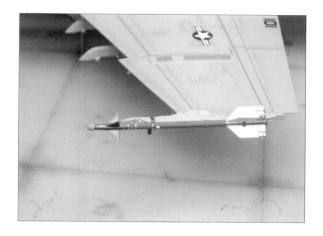

The completed AIM-9L – note how it doesn't sit at the back end of the launch rail. In fact, the kit launch rails are also inaccurate around the rear end. On the real thing, they seem to be block-shaped and flat and had I spotted this before final detailing I would have amended them.

Putty is also used here to make the FOD cushions that slot into each afterburner can – I used metal foil for the handles.

Long shot of the completed Italeri model – complete with stunning Two Bob's decals. Note the creative use of FOD-covers on the intakes.

Finishing off

Needless to say, the Super Hornets weather in just the same way as their predecessors, having a very flat finish, even when they have been deployed at sea for some time. To achieve this effect, I sprayed on Polly Scale's excellent Flat varnish – it goes on easily and dries flat. Once again I used dark grey pastel chalk along the panel lines to bring them to life. In my opinion this is more convincing on modern jets like the Super Hornet than a wash with ink.

FOD guards

I couldn't resist adding these to the afterburner cans. Simply add Blu-Tac putty to each can and a small strip of metal foil for a handle. I used red paint followed by a thin wash using Tamiya Smoke to bring out the creases in the fabric. A touch of matt varnish finishes them off – along with the obligatory RBF tags, that is. Metal foil was used for the main intakes. A little artistic licence was employed here in both design and colour – not to mention the addition of the VFA-41 badges (spare decals from the Two Bobs sheet).

RIGHT A nice close up – note the enhanced panels using grey pastel dust.

BELOW The completed Black Box cockpit really stands out here.

'Topgun' F/A-18A Hornet

Subject:	F/A-18A Hornet, Bu No. 162887, NSAWC Fighter Weapons School – 'Topgun'
Skill level:	Master
Base kit:	Academy, No. 2191
Scale:	1/32
Additional detailing sets used:	Cutting Edge F/A-18A Super Detailed Cockpit (32119) Black Box Exterior update set (32012) Eduard F-18 Hornet placards (32 108) M.V. Products real lens for nose leg light (L 149)

Paints:		
	Xtracolor:	X-403 Interior Grey Matt FS36231 (cockpit interior)
		X-32 RAF Desert Pink (camouflage pattern)
		X-135 Dark Compass Grey FS 36320 (upper surface 'MIG-29' camouflage)
		X-12 Night Black (nose cone, fin tips)
		X-115 USMC Field Green FS 34097 (underside centreline fuselage)
		X-107 Radome Tan FS 33613 (tip of nose cone radome)
		X-8 Red (in-flight refuelling probe)
	Humbrol:	186 red/brown (camouflage pattern)
	Revell:	No.9 Anthracite Black (seat, instrument panels, canopy)
		No.45 khaki (seat back cushion)
	Tamiya:	X-19 Smoke (undercarriage weathering)
		XF-58 Tan (seat cushion)
	Poly Scale:	NATO Tri Black (tyres)
		Flat varnish (overall)
Decals:	Two Bobs Aviation Graphics (32-018)	

Building the cockpit

The Academy cockpit is fine as far as it goes, but with Cutting Edge releasing several resin super-detailed update sets for various Hornets, including the 'A' model, you can push the boundaries of detail much further. All the detail as per the real aircraft is present, including an excellent Martin Baker SJU 5/6A seat with nicely moulded straps and harness. The best feature though is the inclusion of the square avionics bay behind the ejection seat – fully equipped with appropriate boxes and detail. A wire mesh grill is also provided that can be shown folded back, attaching to one side when you display the finished model.

Two Bobs' release of their superb NSAWC 'Topgun' decal sheet was the inspiration to convert the 'C' kit back to an 'A' model, and the Cutting Edge cockpit makes this much easier. There are a few panel changes on either side of the nose and using the very good plans in the back of the stunning *Uncovering the F/A-18A/B/C/D Hornet* book from Daco Publications, this is a straightforward task. The twin, oval-shaped antennae above and immediately behind the canopy are also left off. The other main alteration is to remove the centre

(continued on page 50)

The real aircraft – a picture gallery

ABOVE I just had to include these stunning photographs taken by Ian Sayer that show current F/A-18A NSAWC Aggressor Hornets. (Ian Sayer)

BELOW This shot shows how the deceptive scheme worn in the Two Bobs decals has evolved. (Ian Sayer)

OPPOSITE A nice image illustrating the complex nature of the nose gear – note the big lens that you can replicate using MV model lens products. (Ian Sayer)

I took inspiration from this photo for the centreline fuel tank fitted to the model – notice how the original grey is wearing through. This can be realistically created on your model by careful dry-brushing with light grey paint. Other small details like the red filler caps add a little more interest. (Ian Sayer)

Right main gear unit – see how the large stencils show up on the hydraulic ram – Eduard's pre-painted placards faithfully reproduce these features and simply look fantastic when closely inspected. (Ian Sayer)

I like this image – showing the metallic nature of the afterburner cans and general weathering around the rear fuselage. There are lots of scuffmarks from ground crew boots and maintenance work. Try using a graphite pencil to recreate these. (Ian Sayer)

Some unit badge! The lightning flash and Top Gun Fighter Weapons School logo is nicely printed on the Two Bobs sheet and remains unaltered from the scheme featured on the sheet to October 2003 when Ian shot his pictures. (Ian Sayer)

Notice here the difference between the F/A-18A fin tip arrangement and the 'C' variant in the other builds. Apparently Black Box either have or are producing 'A'-type fins in resin but with a little work you can readily modify the kit items and save a fortune in the process. (Ian Sayer)

Those reheat cans dominate the aft end – note the off-white coloured individual petal inside the nozzle in some contrast to the original items. The item has almost certainly come from an example of the more powerful F404-GE-402 engine. The ceramic coating applied to petals on these engines turns white under extremes of heat. (Ian Sayer)

Canopy open – note the scuffmarks around the LEX / fuselage join and thin wire to help retract and raise the canopy. Pastel dust and graphite pencil dust are ideal for replicating this grime and weathering. (Ian Sayer)

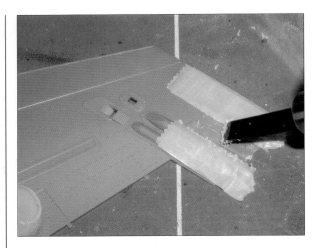

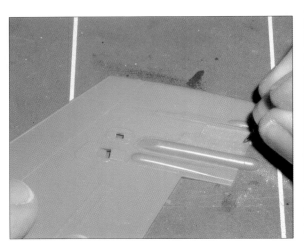

Masking tape is used here to protect the delicately moulded detail at the fin top while the centre fairing is removed for the 'A' arrangement. Again, this is a good opportunity to use the chisel, drawing it across the surface rather than digging in forwards – much easier to control the task.

Any lost rivet detail is quickly reinstated using a small drawing pin. It can be worth drawing pencil lines with a rule to help get each row to line up neatly. Dymo tape is also good for this, cut down into small strips.

fairing of the three that are mounted along the tip of each fin. This is easy if done early – you just need to replace the lost rivets using a small pin. In all other respects the fin looks almost identical to the 'C' fin included in the kit. Note that you will also need to add the three strengthening brackets to the inside base of each fin as these were present on the 'A' Hornets. I really wanted to show this scheme off to its best advantage by having clean lines, and to faithfully represent a typical NSAWC aircraft at rest – maybe one centreline tank and clean wings. The nose cone, airbrake and wings were therefore left closed or unfolded as appropriate. The only concession I allowed was the inclusion of an extended in-flight refuelling probe from Black Box. For what you get, this exterior detail set is very expensive, at least in the UK, so you may not consider the investment worthwhile.

An early task is to scrape away the kit sidewall detail, but the Cutting Edge team have certainly done their homework by building their accessories into the kit. They clearly explain every step of the process and this makes the project so much more enjoyable – unlike some other manufacturers who charge the earth for poorly fitting products. You'll probably find it helpful to refer back to the VFA-86 'Sidewinders' build earlier in this book, as there are some useful build hints there.

In-flight refuelling probe

The inclusion of a nicely moulded in-flight refuelling probe by Black Box in their Exterior Detail set is very welcome. To scratchbuild this item would be a real chore, and the good news is that it all fits together pretty well. You may want to consider the following points. A new resin insert directly replaces the upper portion of the forward fuselage supplied in the kit. The fit to fuselage is quite good if you to line it up carefully, with the resin only needing a slight sanding to blend it in. I gave the part a coat of grey paint to ensure there were no nasty tonal differences in the finished paint job. I noticed that the angle of the front section of the probe wasn't strictly accurate and this necessitated breaking it at the angle and setting it slightly more in-line. The best thing is to look at the photos of the real probe in your references and decide what, if any, corrective action you want to take. Also beware the tiny protruding resin support/wire that emerges from the retraction bay – it is tiny and will almost

In focus: cockpit detailing

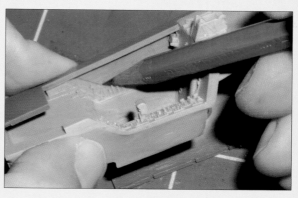

The superb Cutting Edge resin super detail set to help convert the kit's 'C' back to an 'A' type. In fact this manufacturer has several detail sets for the Academy Hornet and they are very well produced – Cutting Edge always seem to do their homework, with the parts fitting accurately.

The resin tub fits perfectly. Dry-fitting first can help you to align the separate side walls and when everything comes together you'll have no horrible errors to correct.

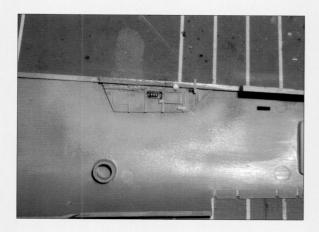

The completed sidewall in place in the left fuselage. Notice the pre-shading giving shadow to the grey surface.

The Cutting Edge acetate dials and faces for the instruments stand out when you add white paint to the reverse face.

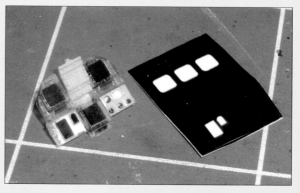

The dials and detail really stand out against the clear plastic kit instrument panel. They need to be masked and then the panel can be sprayed Interior Grey like much of the remainder of the cockpit.

Cutting Edge helpfully include some vinyl masks to protect the faces of the instruments during spraying.

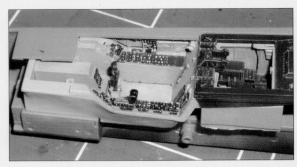

A very nice addition in the Cutting Edge set is the detailed avionics bay that sits immediately behind the pilot. The internal avionics boxes are supplied separately, as is the canvas mesh screen that can be folded aside to view the interior. The screen is supplied in fine wire mesh.

Most of the detail is added to the cockpit and avionics bay, seen installed. Note the careful design of the new tub to fit the top of the nose gear bay.

The cockpit is nearly finished here – just the hose connecting the seat to the rear of the left instrument panel to go. I think the hose is for the pilot's oxygen supply.

Image taken further round showing up the superb resin moulding within the whole cockpit area. The fine detail responds very well to careful dry-brushing and painting.

Around to the right side to give you a full 'walk-around' of the very nearly finished cockpit.

Just visible here behind the ejection seat is the scratched retraction wire mechanism for the canopy made from etched brass and fine fuse wire, all taken from the spares box.

The Black Box in-flight refuelling probe sits in its resin bay that comes as a complete replacement for the kit forward upper fuselage. The fit is quite good, just a little narrower than the cockpit fuselage. This is easily rectified by carefully sanding the join seam, but go easy, as the resin is very soft.

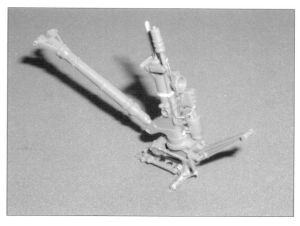

The kit nose gear unit is OK as far as it goes, but in this scale you need to add the lines and tubes that cover the right side of the leg. Contrary to the kit instructions, the nose leg can be inserted afterwards, if you trim the locating pins at the top of the leg.

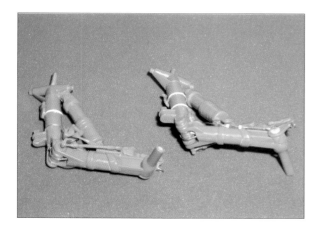

The main gear units also benefit from the super-detail treatment. Fuse wire and tiny strips of lead foil do the trick and make each item look quite busy. When the Tamiya Smoke (X-19) wash is added, the final effect looks convincing.

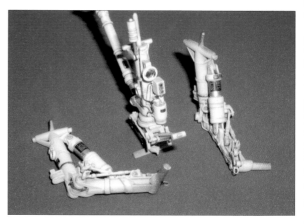

The completed undercarriage units – including the pre-painted Eduard placards that finish them off nicely. Again, these items are all left off until the decaling and underside detailing is finished – thereby avoiding damage.

certainly break off (as mine did, despite some care). The danger occurs when you lay the model on its back for other tasks, as this tiny part makes contact with your work mat. I fail to see why they didn't mould this part separately. To add insult to injury there were holes in the interior of the afterburner cans and the door covering the in-flight refuelling probe. Despite a visit to my supplier all the other sets were variously affected so, again, take care. For all this, the finished probe looks the part and I think adds to the finished model. The probe and door inner face are bright red and I used Xtracolor X-8.

Undercarriage units

The F/A-18 Hornet has a very sturdy, rugged undercarriage. The kit parts are well tooled but you can add additional detail – especially the wiring and hydraulic lines that run the length of all three units. I used fuse wire for this, together with small strips of lead foil, secured with superglue that acted as

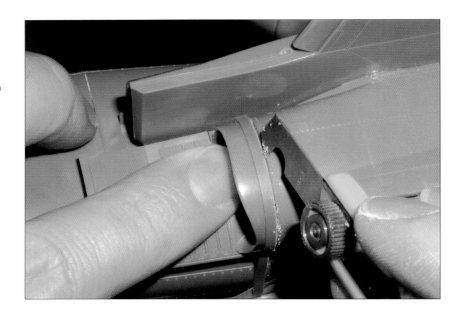

As with the original release, the engine intakes don't fit very well and need some filling. Here the panel lines are being rescribed using an Olfa P-Cutter, guided by Dymo tape. The pin referred to earlier can be used to get into some of those awkward recesses.

bracing bands. Having added the detail you want, you can pre-shade the parts. I sprayed mine enamel gloss black, followed by white. The idea is to ghost on the white and build up the effect you want gradually with several light passes of your airbrush. This will generate shadows and a convincing 3-D effect – so that much more of the detail becomes apparent. When all is dry, you can add Tamiya Smoke (X-19) with a fine brush to all the recesses. This immediately makes the parts spring to life and they are nearly done. The finishing touch is undoubtedly to add the excellent pre-painted Eduard placards. These superb products give an element of finesse that we could never hope to emulate with a brush or any other technique and really make a difference in 1/32nd scale. It is definitely best to leave off the units and tyres until your model is painted and decaled. This way you'll avoid a huge amount of masking and risk of damage to the finished parts. When the time comes, you'll have the option of using the rubber tyres supplied as an option or the plastic ones. The plastic parts have the edge because you can sand slight flats onto the underside to simulate the tyres taking the weight of the aircraft. When it comes to attaching the tyres, I have at last found a use for polystyrene tube cement. It's great because it allows you a few moments to line everything up with the aircraft standing on its undercarriage and you can look at it from every angle to make sure the wheels are at the correct angles.

Other detailing

As with the previous Academy build in this book, there was some re-scribing to be done around the intakes. Also, the excellent Eduard pre-painted etched set provided a real boost to the cockpit and undercarriage units.

Painting

One of the most exciting things about the NSAWC aircraft is the colour scheme that they have worn over the years. The pictures on pages 46–49 of a real Aggressor machine illustrate a scheme that is clearly not the same as in the Two Bobs decal sheet. However, the pictures show good details of the F/A-18A aircraft and an indication of the colours used and how the scheme has developed. Also note the typical stores layout – very sparse, with the real aircraft featured only sporting a centreline 330-gal. tank. How this has weathered is also interesting particularly how the grey has begun to show through. The fin antennae arrangement is also worth noting because this needs to be modified in the Academy kit.

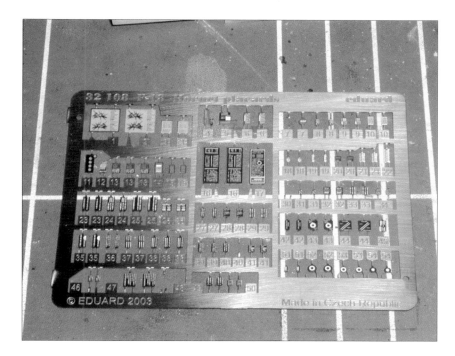

A close up of the Eduard pre-painted placard set – fantastic, and obtaining this level of accuracy is simply unachievable through conventional painting.

The painting task is onerous, and it's worth spending a little time planning how you are going to tackle it. I decided that the best way was to spray the smaller sections first and, when each was dry, to mask it, except for the main camouflage scheme colours of Dark Ghost Grey, RAF Desert Pink and a red/brown colour that was unavailable in the Hannants Xtracolor range. I found a good option in the Humbrol matt range (186). In fact, Two Bobs suggest this in their instruction sheet. For masking, I always use Tamiya masking tape, being the best product on the market. They have now produced a broader tape that helps to cover the large areas involved in this project. The broad tape is particularly low-tack and this helps to ensure you don't remove any paint when taking the tape off. I sprayed the Desert Pink overall first and it took over a tin to finish the job – so make sure you have a spare tin before you start. I also find that by thinning this paint with cellulose thinners it dries ready to mask in 24 hours – pretty good for gloss enamel. Be careful, as ever, to spray in a well-ventilated area with an appropriate particle mask on. The Humbrol brown came next and it went on well.

I almost forgot to check exactly how the decals were printed. This does matter, because several of the decals are two-tone and are designed to lie across the camouflage demarcation line. If you fail to accurately spray the pattern, your decals may end up misplaced. At the very least you may need to respray some areas and this delays everything while the paint dries.

Removing the masks and preparation for decals

When removing the masking tape it is worth being patient. It is all too easy to pull a bit harder or faster, only to ruin a good paint job. The exciting part, though, is that the final scheme is revealed bit by bit. I was always a little sceptical about the impression this 'MIG-29' effect was supposed to have, but it actually works. The more you look at the black/grey fin tips, the black nose section, and especially the grey wing leading edges, the more it gives the impression of a MIG-29 – very clever. I find that whenever I mask between colours, I get a small step in the demarcation line between them. Although very small it is usually enough to spoil the look of any decals that straddle the

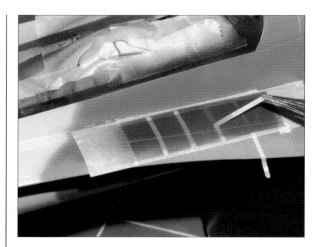

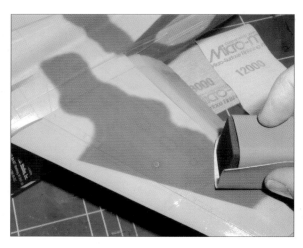

The striped decal located above each LEX seemed a bit too big and so I sprayed the markings instead – thin strips of Tamiya masking tape are used here before the dark grey or black paint is sprayed on.

Micro Mesh is a tremendous invention used to good effect here to remove the tiny raised lines between colours that are created when masking and spraying. You need to wait until the paint is completely dry before attempting any of this work.

change in colour. The problem is easily resolved though by using a strip of Micro Mesh (6000 grade for example) and gently rubbing across the line. Any protrusion is quickly removed and because the fabric is so fine the paintwork is unaffected.

Because the Humbrol paint is matt, you'll need to gloss it. For this I used Humbrol Gloss Cote. I always find that it sprays well and doesn't yellow after time like some other varnishes. In addition, it dries quickly and is ready for decals if left overnight.

The Two Bobs decals are of high quality and go on with ease. I used a small amount of Micro Set and Sol decal softening solutions to help them adhere. The final matt finish was achieved using Poly Scale acrylic varnish.

A feature of 'desert' operations is that the paint weathers. Here I am using pastel dust to highlight the panel lines. Dark grey works quite well, but dark brown is effective too. Test out on an isolated area before starting work on the upper fuselage and wings. You don't really get a second chance with this technique, but the key is to apply less first time and add more if necessary to each panel.

Afterburner/reheat cans

While the main paintwork dries you can attend to the Black Box or kit-supplied reheat/afterburner cans. The resin replacements are nice in that they have the inner lining and outer 12 petals moulded to look separate – typical of the General Electric F-404-GE-400 engines supplied on initial Hornets (like the F/A-18A) or later GE-402. The GE-402 is interesting in that the inner faces of the engine nozzles are coated with a white ceramic material that needs to be replicated if you're modelling a later Hornet. The cans were sprayed Humbrol Metalcote Gunmetal, and this dries very quickly. By lightly buffing the finish with a soft duster you can achieve a nice dark metallic finish – typical of the rear (main) section of Hornet reheat cans. They look even better when you work an orange/brown mix of pastel chalk into the recesses between the petals. The finishing touch is to delicately dry-brush the outer edges of the pastels with a little silver paint. I think straight silver is generally too bright for this task and so I use Miniature Paint's Chain Mail or sometimes Bolt Gun Metal. The cans are attached with superglue in the final stages of completing your project. In the meantime, the two large holes in the rear of the fuselage are helpful finger holds – you'll need them as the model gets bigger and heavier!

Canopy

The canopy gets some serious treatment from Cutting Edge in the cockpit superdetail set. The whole of the inside structure is replaced by an excellent resin alternative. It features the lightening holes all along the length of the sill that rises when the canopy is opened. There are some additional small parts too and all these can be attached with superglue ahead of spraying with Revell No. 9 Dark Grey. The clear transparencies are very well moulded and have the characteristic thin, raised mould seam down the length. How to remove this has been shown in the previous Hasegawa F/A-18C build. Briefly though, removal is achieved by gentle sanding with a nail buffer and then polished using MER automobile polish. You may want to use a specialist modelling polish, but my small can of automobile polish has lasted about 10 years and is still over half full. Once polished, gently wash the clear parts in warm soapy water and dry off. However, one last task that I think really sets the finished canopies off is to drill out the rivets all along the edges of the clear windscreen and canopy. You can use the trusty pin vice drill with a 0.3mm drill bit.

The kit HUD is replaced using small sections of 35mm transparency film cut to size and attached with Micro Kristal Kleer.

Accentuating the canopy rivet detail makes a real difference when the model is sprayed up – try it! When you look at Hornet canopies close up the rivet detail is pretty noticeable, especially when the aircraft have been at sea and collected grime and dirt on operations.

ABOVE AND BELOW The completed model looks impressive – uncluttered to show off the stunning paint scheme. And if you like this Aggressor scheme, why not try the alternative offered on the Two Bobs sheet, featuring the grey, blue and white SU-27 Flanker lookalike?

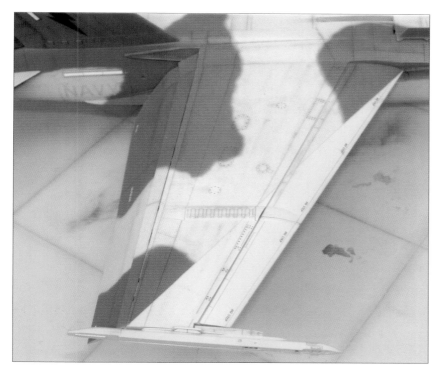

LEFT The Ghost Grey leading edge markings help creates the illusion of a different shaped wing and aircraft – potentially critical in air-to-air engagements. It is also a nice feature of this particular scheme.

BELOW I like this picture showing the weathering and overall marking arrangement around the rear of the airframe. You can just make out the pastel staining around the rudder hinge points – another area prone to weathering and marking on the F/A-18.

ABOVE The dropped flap option in any F/A-18 kit is a must for Hornet scale modellers – sadly lacking on the Italeri offering, but nicely done here by Academy and Hasegawa in their kits. It is worth attaching the flaps with superglue because it is all too easy to break them when handling this 'beast'!

RIGHT The earlier problems with the fit of the left LEX are left behind now the aircraft is finished. This is an area suitable for some weathering – especially around the vents.

Special modelling ideas

Display bases

Why display your completed model on a display base at all? Well, there are a few reasons. Firstly, just take any model show or convention; look at the difference between models on a decent base and those either on poor bases or, worse, no base at all – there is just no comparison. For me, the aim is to try to set the finished model off, in its natural habitat. It is important not to over-complicate the base, or else you run the risk of distracting the onlooker from your model.

There are a number of specialist manufacturers that produce purpose-built display bases for scale models. The neat diorama by Ian Taylor featuring an F/A-18A Hornet about to launch from a carrier deck's angled catapult is a case in point. Note the raised blast shield, 'active' crewmembers and deck colour that is close to Gunship Grey.

Another model that caught my eye is Jonathan Burns's F/A-18A in 1/72nd scale. Note the folded wing tips, raised air brake and yellow deck tractor unit. Jonathan has used a simple and cheap printed card base from Verlinden and glued it onto a suitable wooden board. You can often get ready-made boards (like kitchen chopping boards) from hardware stores, and these are worth checking out. The addition of these small accessories can add real interest to your finished model and is so much more rewarding than simply viewing the model alone.

MDF board (available in the UK) is made from a sort of crushed wood/paper/resin pulp, and comes in different sizes. It is ideal because it can be cut and shaped using wood routing tools but be careful to use an appropriate facemask, as the particles are toxic. One of the benefits of this type of board is that it has a smooth finish, unlike woodchip for example, which is a bit too rough to be used.

Step 1: base colour   Spray the base in the appropriate colour for the surface you are seeking to replicate – in this case, concrete. Aeromaster even produce a light grey paint called 'Old Concrete' which is ideal.

Step 2: additional detailing   Decide if you want any grass or other textures – this can help break up the look and adds interest. Any good hobby- or model-supplies retailer should stock all sorts of grass, ground soils and greenery. Don't go overboard though – unless you are creating a full diorama. After all, you are trying to show off your completed model.

Step 3: marking out concrete/taxi routes   When the main base colour is dry, you can start to measure up the squares that make up the huge slabs of concrete used in most modern aircraft hard-standing areas. Mark out the squares using a soft graphite pencil and rule. It's really important to look at pictures of parked F/A-18s and notice what markings are typical for the hard-standing areas. There are invariably yellow taxi route lines and even large numbers and letters denoting specific parking bays and the like. The taxi routes are best sprayed on, and broad Tamiya tape or other less expensive masking tape should suffice. Remove the tape as soon as you've sprayed to help reduce the possibility of lifting paint from the base layer.

Step 4: create shadows/weathering   This is important, as it really brings the base to life. Spray Tamiya Smoke (X-19) along the pencil lines you've used to mark out the concrete squares. One pass of the airbrush is usually enough as you don't want to exaggerate the effect. Oil drops and hydraulic spills are frequent beneath parked aircraft and you can use Tamiya Smoke or small amounts of the oil you get on top of unstirred enamel paint. Apply sparingly

RIGHT AND BELOW RIGHT
Ian Taylor's neat diorama in
1/144th scale – how does he do it?
Ian is known for incorporating
insane levels of detail in this scale,
such as moving canopies.

using a small, fine brush. Cracks in the concrete on actual aircraft hard-standings
are common, and I use a fine graphite pencil for these – again, take a look at the
pictures in reference books and magazines for examples. Final weathering can be
achieved using pastel chalks, dusted on and worked into the surface. Browns,
oranges and yellow all have a place in this process and a bit of artistic licence can
work wonders.

A detail from Jonathan Burns'
F/A-18 Hornet diorama.

ABOVE This time Jonathan Burns has produced a very realistic
setting for his F/A-18A Hornet, using a card base from Verlinden
to really set the model off. This does make all the difference to a
finished model display and is also a very cost-effective option.

BELOW This nice model by Roger Brown from Harrow Scale
Model Club in the UK is very neat – taking the low-vis markings
from the Academy kit. The stores selection and open canopy
greatly add interest to his finished model.

Grey camouflage weathering

Both the Light (FS 36375) and Dark (FS 36320) Compass (Ghost) Greys are prone to significant weathering – especially when the Hornet is at sea. The deck and maintenance crews work hard at preventing corrosion and this means using fresh paint, sprayed along affected panel lines and other worn areas. This new paint can take on a lighter or darker appearance depending on the light conditions and whether it goes on over the darker of lighter base colour applied to the aircraft. As ever, a successful finish will come via good research – looking at as many pictures (preferably colour ones) of the F/A-18 Hornet and studying where the touch-up paint gets added. Getting this effect to look right in model form is quite a challenge. Using a paintbrush doesn't look right most of the time so the airbrush is needed. The technique I use isn't as daunting as it may at first seem. The key is well-thinned paint sprayed at very low pressure (maybe 5/6 lb per sq. in.), very close to the surface of your Hornet model. You do of course need a decent compressor with adjustable air pressure – compressed air cans are not an option. I also find this technique easier using my Badger 150 double-action airbrush (the air flow and paint flow can be adjusted using the same sliding trigger).

When you think you're ready, test out the flow of paint on a piece of white scrap card – you'll be able to see what effect you're going to achieve and exactly how much paint is going on. By gently drawing back the trigger the paint begins to flow, but keep the airbrush on the move – it is very easy to cause a pooling of paint if you are stationary for even a second. A certain amount of confidence is needed – after all, you are spraying onto the main paint finish. But don't worry, it is very easy to return with the base colour later and over spray any effect you aren't happy with. The accompanying pictures should provide some more guidance.

Hornet-specific weathering

I thought it might be useful to point out one or two areas on the Hornet that seem to attract particular weathering effects.

1. Between the fins. There are two small holes on top of the fuselage near the front of each fin root. At first I thought they may have been fuel dump outlets, but then I used some common sense – the fuel outlets are at the rear edge of the fin tips, well away from the volatile jet exhausts. They almost always seem to stream a yellowish residue back towards the jet pipes. Yellow or light orange pastel chalk dust applied using a very fine brush can produce this effect.

2. Hydraulic fluid and hot gas streaking. This is usually a dark brown or grey colour and is very noticeable trailing back from the hinge attachment points above and below the wings where the leading edge slats mate to the main centre wing sections; back from the rudder hinge positions; on the undersides aft of the main gear bays. In the latter case the streaking is usually very marked. The longer the machine has been on patrol, the more marked the weathering. Canadian Air Force Hornets are very prone to all these weathering effects.

Using pastels to enhance panel lines and rivet detail

First, ensure that only c.2mm of bristle protrudes from the stock of the pastel brush. Rub this lightly across the pastel stick and shake off the excess. Draw the bristles firmly across the panel lines. I normally need to recharge the brush after every couple of inches or so. Blow away any excess pastel dust when you finish each small section. You can just see the effect taking shape and it can be very convincing. In many respects this technique is an alternative to pre-shading that involves spraying black paint along all the panel lines before the model takes the main camouflage colours. I think pre-shading works best

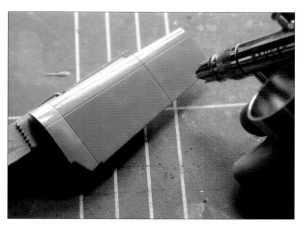

ABOVE AND RIGHT By using your airbrush at a very low setting (c. 6psi) great control is gained when trying to add the touch-up paint so often seen on not just Hornet aircraft but all other US carrier-borne machines.

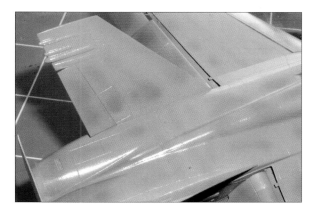

The base colour for this TUDM F/A-18D is Gunship Grey. Here I've used darker and lighter shades of Xtracolor gloss enamel paint to create a weathered finish.

Between the fins – notice the weathering from pastels and yellowish streaking from the small vents. This whole area frequently gets very worn and grubby from the ground crew members climbing all over it. I have been restrained here but you can go to town with confidence.

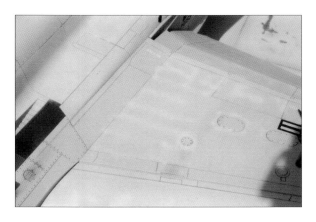

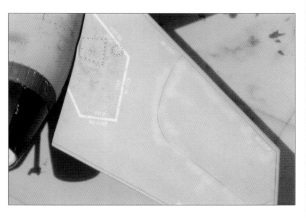

ABOVE AND RIGHT You can just about see the final effects of all the hard work adding touch-up paint to key areas of the airframe. The effect adds greatly to any finished Hornet model and is almost a 'must-do'.

Just notice the heavy hydraulic fluid stains streaking back on the upper wings at the break in the leading edge slats – and elsewhere!

when you use acrylics for the main scheme – ghosting on the top coats until you get the required 'see-through' effect. I mostly use enamels that are dense and saturated; the pre shading is easily covered and you only need to then add further weathering later. It is also worth taking one or two of the scale-model magazines, like *Tamiya Model Magazine International* and *Fine Scale Modeler* as these regularly feature 'how-to' features and develop some of the techniques covered in this chapter.

Some interesting projects to try

In this section there are a number of photographs showing some interesting Hornet subjects, for those looking for inspiration and ideas for special effects when finishing the model. Mark Attrill's pictures of the Canadian Air Force CF-18A Hornets are quite unique; the challenge here is to try to track down an appropriate decal sheet – or try out some fantastically complicated masking. Either way, a well-finished model in any of these schemes could be a showstopper.

I recently saw a fantastic model of an F/A-18A Hornet by Neil Burkill on the excellent Aircraft Resource Centre website. His finishing is second to none and Neil's CAG bird from VFA-113 'Stingers' built from the Hasegawa kit is truly stunning, particularly his attention to detail in the weathered finish. Neil used oil paints to weather much of the airframe, with the wash collecting in the rivets and panel lines to produce a highly realistic effect. If you plan to do this, I suggest you use brown/grey ink; this is much better than black, which is simply too dark and contrasts greatly, and unrealistically, with the light greys used on most Hornets.

ABOVE AND LEFT One of the most effective ways of weathering light-coloured paint on aircraft is to choose a slightly darker shade of the base colour in pastel – added here using a small stubby brush.

ABOVE AND BELOW Wow, what a scheme! The Royal Canadian Air Force certainly know how to impress – now all we need to do is find a decal sheet. (Mark Attrill)

ABOVE A Swiss Air Force F/A-18C Hornet in Tiger livery (seen at Tiger Meet, 2004) – very unusual for Swiss Hornets, which usually appear quite drab. (Ian Sayer)

BELOW Another view of the same Swiss Hornet, this time taxiing past Ian's lens. Note the colourful 'Tiger' Sidewinder air-to-air missiles. (Ian Sayer)

RIGHT The Academy F/A-18C finished with wings folded and air-to-air missiles attached. This always adds interest – especially when you include the wing-fold option.

BELOW Adding detail and weathering to key areas of your model, such as the area of the centreline tank, will really help in obtaining a satisfactory result.

ABOVE This shot illustrates how busy you can make your finished Hornet. You can add interest by raising the canopy; folding the radome/radar nose cone; and folding the wing tips.

BELOW It's worth paying attention to detail – especially when modelling Hornets in 1/32nd scale. Note here the MV lens and coloured lights on the nose undercarriage unit. Note too the pastel weathering around the panel lines, which breaks up the main paint colours.

ABOVE Chosing colourful decals – usually associated with the CAG (Commander Air Group) aircraft – can add great interest, as illustrated here on the Academy F/A-18C in VFA-86 'Sidewinders' markings.

BELOW The use of decal setting solutions like Micro Sol and Set are essential to make sure any markings settle down completely over the moulded-in detail. Hopefully, the black 'Top Gun' unit marking here looks like it's been painted on.

Further reading, media and websites

Key publications

Coremans, Danny and Deboeck, Nico *Boeing F/A-18A/B/C/D Hornet*
    (Daco Publications, 2004)
Davis, Greg and Neill, Chris *Walk Around F/A-18 Hornet* (Squadron Signal
    Publications, 1999)
Holmes, Tony *US Navy Hornet Units of Operation Iraqi Freedom (Part One)*,
    Combat Aircraft No. 46 (Osprey Publishing Ltd, 2004)
Kinzey, Bert *In Detail & Scale Vol 69*: *F/A-18E & F/A-18F Super Hornet*
    (Squadron Signal Publications, 2004)
Peeters, Willy and Brooks, John *Lock On No. 15: F/A-18 A/C & CF-18C Hornet*
    (Verlinden Productions, 1992)
World Air Power Journal *McDonnell Douglas F/A-18 Hornet* (Autumn/Fall 1996,
    Vol.26 p.50-111)

Just a selection of the many references that are available – notably the Verlinden *Lock-On* guide focusing on the 'A' and 'C' variants of the Hornet.

Squadron Signal also produce the *Walk Around* guide on the Hornet and Super Hornet with some very useful drawings and unique images.

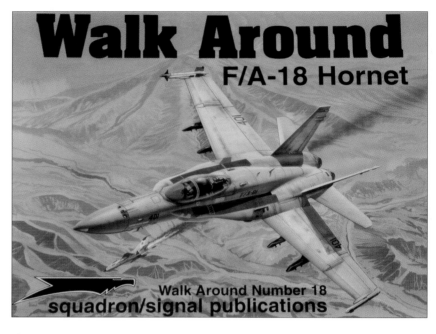

Walk Around
F/A-18 Hornet

Walk Around Number 18
squadron/signal publications

Other publications and articles

Aeroguide 20: *McDonnell Douglas F-18A Hornet* (Linewrights Ltd., 1988)

Boyer, Paul *Hasegawa's new "Super Bug"* (Fine Scale Modeler, April 2004, Vol.22 No.4 p.60–61)

Braybrook, Roy *F/A-18 Hornet* (Osprey Aerospace, 1991)

Classic Aircraft Series No.14 *Tomcat vs Hornet, An Air Forces Special* (Key Publishing)

Drendel, Lou *F/A-18 Hornet in Action No.136* (Squadron Signal Publications, 1993)

Evans, Andy *Boeing F/A-18E/F Super Hornet and EA-18 Growler* (Scale Aircraft Modelling, September 2003, Vol. 25 No.7 p.442–454)

Evans, Andy *Boeing (McDonnell Douglas) F/A-18 Hornet 'Bugs' abroad – overseas operators* (Scale Aircraft Modelling, December 2003, Vol. 25 No.10 p.658–670)

Evans, Andy *Boeing (McDonnell Douglas) F/A-18A/B/C/D in US service: America's first generation Hornets* (Scale Aircraft Modelling, May 2004, Vol. 26 No. 3 p.149–160)

Isby, David C. *How to Fly and Fight in the F/A-18 Hornet* (Harper Collins Publishers, 1997)

Ripley, Tim *Air War Bosnia – UN and NATO Air Power* (Airlife Publishing Ltd, 1996)

Schramm, Larry *Academy's F/A-18C Hornet* (Fine Scale Modeler, September 2003, Vol. 21 No.7 p.22–27)

Useful websites

www.aircraftresourcecenter.com   Very good for photographic reference and scale model builds/galleries of completed models.

www.F-4dablemodels.com   Excellent references for TUDM F/A-18D Hornets in Royal Malaysian Air Force service – good newsletter, decals and accessories to complete your Hornet.

www.twobobs.net   Originators of fantastic decals for F/A-18E/F Super Hornets.

www.hannants.co.uk   The best model kit and accessory international mail order company in the UK – handy if you do not have your own supplier locally.

An indispensable reference for the F/A-18F build or indeed the single-seat 'E' kit – Squadron Signal's *In Detail* and *Scale* reference. It contains a useful scale-modelling section at the end, and again, is a must for building the Super Bug.

The timing by Daco Publications of this awesome book was perfect. There are references and *references* – and this is one you simply must have! The Daco Publications walkaround reference guide is simply the most useful purchase you can make as an F/A-18 Hornet scale modeller.

www.hyperscale.com   If you haven't heard of this site, check it out today for reviews, discussion, scale model galleries and a whole lot more.

www.meteorprod.com   This is where you can find out all about the excellent Cutting Edge resin sets for the F/A-18 Hornet – plus a lot more.

www.boeing.com/defense-space/military/fa18 photos.htm   Some very useful data from the manufacturers; plus pictures and other info.

www.voodoo.cz/hornet/   Some great Hornet pics here – worth checking out.

www.student.net/customasp/axl/plane   Again, some good pictures and Hornet galleries – ideal for reference and inspiration.

www.ipms-uk.co.uk   Getting better all the time as a valuable resource for all kinds of information including: Special Interest Groups (SIGs), international branch and club networks, and info on the biggest scale modelling event on the planet – Scale Model World.

www.etchmate.com   Source of the fantastic etched-metal folding tool used in this book.

www.finescale.com   A good discussion forum and point of reference.

Kits available

Full kits

The aim here is to list the current availability of F/A-18 Hornet models, their scales, plus some of the pros and cons of each. Even a cursory glance at the Hornet kit listing here indicates the dominance of Hasegawa as the primary F/A-18 manufacturer. No less than eleven F/A-18 kits are shown as currently available in 1/72nd, 1/48th and 1/32nd scales. The next most prolific producers are Revell and Italeri, both with five either currently available or planned for release in the near future. Academy have of course produced their stunning F/A-18C and this has now been released in two different schemes and boxes. The pros and cons of the Academy, Italeri and Hasegawa offerings have already been discussed in the separate builds, and so I won't repeat the information here.

Manufacturer F/A-18 variant and scale

	F/A-18A	F/A-18B	F/A-18C	F/A-18D	F/A-18E	F/A-18F
Academy			32 (x 2)	32 [2]		
Airfix	72					
Hasegawa	32 [1]	48	72 (x 2) 48	72, 48	72 (x 2)	72 (x 2)
Italeri			72	72	72, 48	48
Minicraft	72 (x 2)					
Panda			32 [2]	32 [2]	144	144 (x 2)
Revell Monogram			144, 72	144	48 [2]	48 [2]
Testors	48					

Notes
(x 2) = number of kits available from manufacturer in that scale
[1] Prototype version
[2] Due for release during 2004/5

1/72nd and 1/144th scales

In terms of sheer quality and refinement, Revell and Hasegawa between them have probably got 1/72nd scale wrapped up with their excellent tooling of the F/A-18C, D, E and F (especially the latter E and F). In fact these manufacturers collaborate on a regular basis, with the same or similar products common to each being released in each other's boxes. You may wish to check this when purchasing. Before leaving the smallest scale, 1/144th, it is interesting to note that a relatively new manufacturer to many scale modellers, Panda, is ready to 'enter the Hornet's nest' by releasing kits of the Super Hornet. Strangely, Hannants also has listed 1/32nd scale releases by this manufacturer of the 'C' and 'D' – very curious, considering that we now have the outstanding kits from Academy.

F/A-18C HORNET

■ Various weapons included   ■ Solid synthetic-rubber tires   ■ Fully engraved panel lines & rivet details
■ Die-cast metal landing gear struts   ■ Accurately reproduced exterior and cockpit
■ Open or closed canopy, radome & airbrake
■ Lifelike four figures included;two pilots and two ground crews

ACADEMY
HOBBY MODEL KITS

1/32nd

1/48th scale

Hasegawa are the clear market leaders here, with excellent models of both the single seat F/A-18C and two seat F/A-18D Legacy Hornets. Both these models have been featured, with a very different approach taken to each build. The 'C' tries to illustrate the use of limited etched-metal additions and aftermarket decals, with the real focus on achieving that US Navy jet weathering so typical of carrier-borne aircraft. The 'D' has been particularly rewarding in terms of the finished result.

Sadly the only quarter-scale offerings of the F/A-18E and 'F' at the time of writing have been the kits from Italeri. Its shortcomings are described in detail starting on page 35. But no book on building the Hornet would be complete without the model being included so I've done my best with a difficult offering.

The exciting news is that Revell/Monogram are about to release up to date offerings of the Super Hornet in 1/48th scale, so you will at least have an alternative to the Italeri kit. I've covered the very good Black Box resin cockpit and other details that you can use as part reference for when you get stuck into your box of plastic.

1/32nd scale

There are no prizes for guessing who has captured the 1/32nd scale F/A-18 market – yes, it's Academy. They currently produce two kits of the F/A-18C, with a proposed release of the two-seat 'D' sometime during 2004/5. This kit has already been described in detail previously, being converted back to an F/A-18A of the NSAWC 'Aggressor' squadron in one build. This incorporated one of the superb Cutting Edge resin detail sets combined with the fantastic decals from Two Bobs. It would have been great to include the 'SU-27 Flanker' lookalike scheme also contained on the sheet, but alas time ran out.

I've had several conversations with fellow modellers that have bought one of the Academy F/A-18s, but they say they're afraid to start them because they

The superb 1/32nd-scale Academy kit box top showing the COs F/A-18C of VFA-192. This is now available, interestingly, as a second release featuring the VFA-105 'Gunslingers' machine covered in the 1/48th-scale Hasegawa build.

No. 2619 | 1:48 | **F/A-18F** SUPERHORNET TWINSEATER
MODEL KIT/MODÈLE RÉDUIT SCALE/ÉCHELLE

ABOVE Italeri's packaging of the F/A-18F Hornet – a kit soon to be overtaken in importance by Revell/Monogram when their F/A-18 Super Hornets are launched.

may spoil such a big and valuable kit. This is a real shame and I would urge you to get the kit out of the loft or attic and start building – it is nowhere near as daunting as the contents may appear on opening the box – and I have been lucky enough to save my pennies and build two now! Academy even includes tiny screws and a screwdriver to help secure everything together. Academy's decals are fine and can be used. All these options can combine to enable you to build a real showstopper.

Detail sets and decals

Full details of all accessories used to complete the projects in this book are given at the beginning of each build. A complete listing of everything available for the F/A-18 Hornet scale modeller would rapidly fall out of date and has therefore not been provided here. Check out your local supplier or one of the big mail order suppliers.

Index

Figures in **bold** refer to illustrations

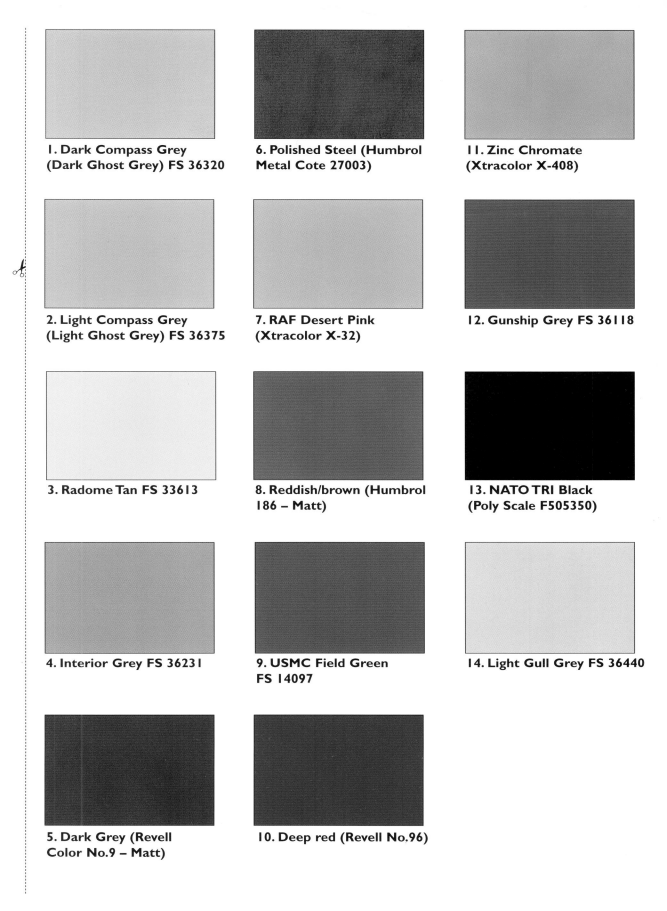

1. Dark Compass Grey
(Dark Ghost Grey) FS 36320

6. Polished Steel (Humbrol
Metal Cote 27003)

11. Zinc Chromate
(Xtracolor X-408)

2. Light Compass Grey
(Light Ghost Grey) FS 36375

7. RAF Desert Pink
(Xtracolor X-32)

12. Gunship Grey FS 36118

3. Radome Tan FS 33613

8. Reddish/brown (Humbrol
186 – Matt)

13. NATO TRI Black
(Poly Scale F505350)

4. Interior Grey FS 36231

9. USMC Field Green
FS 14097

14. Light Gull Grey FS 36440

5. Dark Grey (Revell
Color No.9 – Matt)

10. Deep red (Revell No.96)

11. Zinc Chromate (Xtracolor X-408)

Ideal for painting the so-called 'Slime Lights' (formation lights). These lights are invariably provided as yellow decals in the kits but that yellow is too bright. Zinc Chromate yellow is much nearer the correct shade.

12. Gunship Grey FS 36118

Used as the overall camouflage colour for Royal Malaysian Air Force (TUDM) F/A-18Ds. The aircraft weather in service so try adding a little white to the base colour and spray into the main panels.

13. NATO TRI Black (Poly Scale F505350)

A very useful dark grey colour for the rubber tyres on the Hornet. Used as the base colour, it is then lightened considerably by dabbing light grey pastel chalk all over the tyre surface when dry.

14. Light Gull Grey FS 36440

Good match for the tip of the nose cone radome on TUDM F/A-18Ds. This suggestion comes from Jason Cheah and his colleagues who have examined the real aircraft.

6. Polished Steel (Humbrol Metal Cote 27003)

Good for the reheat cans themselves and the band immediately forward of the cans. This paint sprays easily and can be buffed up to create several metallic tones.

7. RAF Desert Pink (Xtracolor X-32)

This forms the basis of one of the main upper surface camouflage colours used on NSAWC Aggressor F/A-18A Hornets. It weathers down to a lighter shade of the base colour.

8. Reddish/brown (Humbrol 186 – Matt)

The second main camouflage colour for NSAWC Aggressor Hornets. This dark reddish/brown seems to fade in the bright desert sunlight. It can be useful to lightly spray desert sand over some the upper surface panels to achieve a weathered look.

9. USMC Field Green FS 14097

The Aggressor scheme used for the 'master build' F/A-18A Hornet is designed to confuse the enemy by making the aircraft look like a MIG-29. A small narrow section of the underside centreline is painted Field Green.

10. Deep red (Revell No.96)

Although slightly metallic, this colour is a good match for the Two Bob's decal sheet colour used on the VFA-41 Black Aces F/A-18F. Only applied to the fin tips and FOD engine intake covers used in the project.

1. Dark Compass Grey (Dark Ghost Grey) FS 36320

Main camouflage colour for upper surfaces on US F/A-18 Hornets and F/A-18E/F Super Hornets. Weathers considerably when aircraft at sea. Often seen with small touching up, often in lighter or darker shades of the base colour.

2. Light Compass Grey (Light Ghost Grey) FS 36375

Main undersurface camouflage colour for US Navy and Marine Corps Hornets and Super Hornets. As with upper surfaces, the colour weathers in the same way as FS 36320.

3. Radome Tan FS 33613

As the name suggests, this is the colour used on the majority of US Hornets. Note that the TUDM F/A-18D aircraft featured in the 'advanced build' chapter has a radome tip colour nearer Light Gull Grey FS 36440.

4. Interior Grey FS 36231

The main cockpit interior colour for F/A-18s. Most of the dials and instrument panels are dark grey and contrast heavily with this much lighter base colour.

5. Dark Grey (Revell Color No.9 – Matt)

This is a good choice for the 'black' areas of the cockpit. This paint looks about right for inside the canopy, cockpit sills and ejection seats. Also useful for the reheat/afterburner cans as described in some of this book's projects.